Organizations and their members:
a contingency approach

Harper & Row's series in organization and management

JAY LORSCH, general editor

Organizations and their members:
a contingency approach

JAY W. LORSCH
Professor of Organizational Behavior
Graduate School of Business Administration
Harvard University, Boston

JOHN J. MORSE
Associate Professor of Organizational Behavior
Graduate School of Management
University of California, Los Angeles

HARPER & ROW, PUBLISHERS
New York, Evanston, San Francisco, London

Information appearing in Fig. 3.5 and data on page 153 were taken from HUMAN INFORMATION PROCESSING: INDIVIDUALS AND GROUPS FUNCTIONING IN COMPLEX SOCIAL SITUATIONS, by Harold M. Schroder, Michael R. Driver, and Siegfried Streufert. Copyright © 1967 by Holt, Rinehart & Winston, Inc. Reprinted by permission of Holt, Rinehart & Winston, Inc.

Sponsoring Editor: *John Greenman*
Project Editor: *Carol E. W. Edwards*
Designer: *Frances Torbert Tilley*
Production Supervisor: *Stefania J. Taflinska*

ORGANIZATIONS AND THEIR MEMBERS:
A CONTINGENCY APPROACH

Library of Congress Cataloging in Publication Data

Lorsch, Jay William.
    Organizations and their members.
    (Harper & Row's series in organization and management)
    1. Industrial organization—Case studies.
I. Morse, John J., joint author. II. Title.
HD38.L582   301.18'32   74-8622
ISBN 0-06-044044-9

Contents

Preface

This is a study of people, specifically people working in formal organizations and interacting with the organization's environments. The data were gathered in ten separate organizational units, two each in five large companies. We are grateful to the executives who gave us their permission to study their organizations, and we are especially grateful to the participants in the survey for their time and invaluable assistance. Without them, this book would not have been written.

This study has its roots in the contingency theory of organizations that was developed in *Organization and Environment* by Paul R. Lawrence and Jay W. Lorsch. That work was housed primarily in a sociological framework; its relevant variables were organization characteristics, environmental characteristics, and the fit or congruence of organizations and environments. In developing it, Lorsch shared the belief of John J. Morse that a contingency theory of organizations must deal with psychological characteristics of *people,* as well as characteristics of organizations and environments, if it is to capture the true complexity of organizations and management.

Therefore, working as a team on this book, we have attempted to extend organization contingency theory to include individual organization members. Collaboratively, we have developed theory and methodology in order to test an elaborated contingency theory that encompasses individuals, organization, and environment and that explores implications for the practitioner. This study builds on Lorsch's work on a contingency theory of organizations and environments and on Morse's research studies that attempted to incorporate people into the contingency approach. Combining the special skills each of us brought to this study results in a final product that is truly collaborative and integrative. To underscore this, we decided to list our names as authors alphabetically. The listing in no way signals greater or lesser contribution. Each of us as researchers acknowledges his equal debt and gratitude to the other.

Many professional colleagues provided helpful insights, counsel, and suggestions: William McKelvey, William McWhinney, and Robert Tannenbaum of the University of California at Los Angeles; Chris Argyris, Larry Greiner, and Harry Levinson of Harvard; Edward Lawler of the University of Michigan; and Clayton Alderfer of Yale. For all their comments, we are extremely grateful. We are also indebted to Paul Lawrence for his emotional and intellectual support through the several versions of the manuscript, and we wish to acknowledge our special debt to Renato Tagiuri for his especially detailed and insightful suggestions which were most helpful in shaping the final form of this book.

The financial support for the study reported here was provided by the Division of Research, Harvard University Graduate School of Business Administration; and we are grateful to Richard Walton, its director, for this support.

Finally, several persons provided help in scoring research instruments, in typing the numerous versions of this manuscript, and in developing footnotes. To Connie Bourke, Susan Christiansen, Patricia Riley, Linda Rosenbloom, and Ann Walter, our thanks for what at times must have seemed an endless job.

In spite of all this help and advice, we cheerfully recognize our responsibility for all errors and omissions.

J. W. L.
Boston

J. J. M.
Westwood

Organizations and their members:
a contingency approach

1

Purpose and concepts

Since the 1960s, a major new direction in organization theory has been taken. This perspective, which has been called "a contingency theory of organization" by some of its proponents, has two major characteristics which distinguish it from our prior understanding of human behavior in organizations.[1] First, it has focused on understanding the factors by which some organizations produce more effective results than others. Second, supported by experimental and field data, as well as by theory, the argument has been advanced that there is no single best way to organize for effective results.[2] Rather, the key to organizational effectiveness rests in

[1] Paul R. Lawrence and Jay W. Lorsch first used this term in their book, *Organization and Environment* (Boston: Harvard Business School, Division of Research, 1967).

[2] In addition to Lawrence and Lorsch, the principal proponents of this view have been James Thompson, *Organizations in Action* (New York: McGraw-Hill, 1967); and Joan Woodward, *Industrial Organizations: Theory and Practice* (London: Oxford University Press, 1965). Others with diverse backgrounds have also provided support for this perspective, for example, historian Alfred Chandler, *Strategy and Structure* (Cambridge: The MIT Press, 1962); and social psychologist Harold J. Leavitt, "Some Effects of Certain Communication Patterns on Group Performance," in *Readings in Social Psychology*, 3rd ed., Eleanor Maccoby, et al., eds. (New York: Holt, Rinehart & Winston, 1958).

matching internal organizational characteristics to the demands of the work the organization must perform in achieving its goals. It is in this sense that the new perspective represents a contingency theory. It is concerned with understanding the interdependent relationship among organizational effectiveness, the internal characteristics of the organization, and the nature of the organization's work. The various contributors to this perspective differ in the ways by which they have conceptualized and/or measured internal organizational characteristics and the work of the organization. For example, Woodward focused on a variety of types of technology as the work variable and regarded formal organizational characteristics as the internal organizational attributes.[3] Lawrence and Lorsch conceptualized the organization's work as dealing with its external environment and viewed the important internal organizational parameters as differentiation, integration, and conflict resolution.[4] Thompson has been concerned with both technology and environment, as well as with a different set of organizational variables (e.g., structure, discretion, and control).[5] We do not intend to dwell on these variations here, since they are of minor importance when compared to the convergence around the major themes mentioned above.

What should be emphasized at the outset is what we regard as a major limitation of the contingency approach as it has been developed so far. The contingent relationship studied and discussed has been between organizational variables and task characteristics; thus, the focus has been primarily one of fitting organizational characteristics to the nature of the work which must be accomplished. Little attention has been paid to the way in which the personal characteristics of organization members are related to organizational factors and the nature of the organization's work when organizations produce effective results.[6] As Duncan has indicated there is a clear need to do this:

> Most contingency theories now tend to be one-sided in that they focus on the characteristics of the environment . . . while ignoring an equally important contingent factor of individual differences among organization members. It

[3] Woodward, *Industrial Organizations.*
[4] Lawrence and Lorsch, *Organization.*
[5] Thompson, *Organizations in Action.*
[6] The one exception to this statement is found in Thompson, *Organizations in Action,* p. 96. However, his treatment of organization members has been limited to suggesting how power processes are used to negotiate a favorable inducements-contributions contract between the organization and its members. Consequently, his view of man is as a rational actor; and he does not consider the range of individual characteristics which are necessary to adequately understand how the nature of organization members can be connected to the organizational and task variables.

is only by beginning to focus on these individual differences that we can begin to develop our contingency theory more fully.[7]

Goals of the Study

The major purpose of our study is to explore how the personal characteristics of organization members can be brought into the contingency theory of organizations. It is necessary to understand how members' personality predispositions are related to organizational and work variables, and to the accomplishment of organizational purposes. The importance of including the nature of organization members in the contingency conceptual framework seems apparent from both a theoretical and practical perspective. From a theoretical viewpoint it is clear that any understanding of how organizations function must include an understanding of how each organizational member is induced to do the organization's work. If a match between particular organizational characteristics and the demands of the organization's work are related to effective organizational performance, it is reasonable to assume that somehow this also has an impact on organization members' willingness to work toward the organization's goals. For it is only through the collective efforts of its members that an organization can produce results.

For the practitioner there is little question that this issue is also critical. Even a quick perusal of daily newspapers, magazines, and business journals produces evidence that many managements are encountering difficulties in encouraging organization members to work effectively toward organization goals.[8-11] Younger employees are reportedly seeking careers which are meaningful in a social, political, and cultural sense; increasingly, they are questioning profit as a motive for the firm's existence, and money as an incentive for themselves.[12] Further, organization members are finding a

[7] Robert Duncan, "Characteristics of Organizational Environments and Perceived Environmental Uncertainty," *Administrative Science Quarterly*, 17 (September 1972): 326.

[8] "Young Workers Found Restless," *The New York Times*, December 6, 1972, p. 34.

[9] "H. E. W. Study Finds Job Content is Hurting Nation," *The New York Times*, December 22, 1972, p. 1.

[10] "Work in America: A Special Section," *Atlantic Monthly* (October 1971):60-104.

[11] Judson Gooding, "Blue-Collar Blues on the Assembly Line," *Fortune* 82 (July 1970):68-71.

[12] James H. Binns, "Principled, Participant Management," *Conference Board Record*, 5 (December 1968):23-26.

variety of ways to meet their material needs so that they have become increasingly concerned with finding personal fulfillment at work. While there has been a flurry of popular interest in these issues in the 1970s, such concerns on the part of managers and students of organization are not new, as is shown by Elton Mayo's writings and the pioneering work of Roethlisberger and Dickson at the Hawthorne works of the Western Electric Company.[13-14] Thus, the problem of stimulating organization members to work toward organizational goals has been important in the past, is of great concern today, and is likely to be so in the future.

While our primary purpose is to explore how the individual characteristics of organization members can be included in a contingency theory of organizations, we have two secondary objectives which also should contribute to this new perspective about organizations. Our first is to more carefully explore how a match between organizational and work variables is connected to organizational effectiveness. The second is to expand the range of organizational variables included in such a conceptual scheme. The importance of these secondary goals will become apparent as we examine those elements of the prior contingency approaches which are relevant to our primary goal of bringing the individual into this theoretical perspective.

Organization and External Environment

As mentioned above, there are several minor variations on the major themes of a contingency approach. The particular contingency theory framework upon which we shall build is that of Lawrence and Lorsch.[15] The reason underlying our choice—beyond our personal predilections for their ideas—is that Lawrence and Lorsch provide insight into the relationship which exists between the internal characteristics of particular functional units (e.g., sales or manufacturing) and the nature of the work in which they are engaged. This is important because if one has a central concern with organization members and how their individual characteristics relate to other variables in contingency theory, what goes on in the func-

---

[13] Elton Mayo, *Human Problems of an Industrial Civilization* (New York: Macmillan, 1933).

[14] F. J. Roethlisberger and William Dickson, *Management and the Worker* (Cambridge: Harvard University Press, 1939).

[15] Lawrence and Lorsch, *Organization*.

tional unit becomes critical. While the division of labor in organizations can take place along product and/or territorial, as well as functional lines, in most organizations the functional unit tends to be the basic building block around which product and territorial units are formed. For example, within most product divisions there are several functional units.[16] Further, we have observed that these functional bases seem important in shaping the career identities of many organizational members, who tend to think of themselves as sales managers, engineers, manufacturing men, researchers, etc. It is within functional units that most organization members closely engage in the organization's work; consequently, it is here that individual, organizational, and work variables interact most intensively. Therefore, while Lawrence and Lorsch's contingency theory deals with a wide spectrum of organizational issues, we shall review only those aspects of their study concerned with the internal characteristics of functional units in relation to the work they must perform.

At the most general level, Lawrence and Lorsch view organizations as open systems constantly interacting with their external environments. An organization's external environment consists of a body of knowledge and information which organization members must absorb and act upon if the organization is to achieve its goals. In the industrial organizations that will be our focus, the external environment consists of information about market, technological, economic, and scientific factors relevant to the organization's purpose of profitable operation. In describing such information as being external to the organization, we are drawing a conceptual boundary around the human system, that is, the organization. Therefore, even though the source of particular information may be physically located in the organization (e.g., production technology, scientific experiments, market research data), we think of it as constituting the *external environment* since this information forms the context in which organization members must reach decisions and act upon them. To make this definition more concrete, we can use, for example, the external environment facing the manufacturing unit of a typical industrial firm. The information which would constitute such a unit's external environment might involve data about production costs, quality of products produced, scheduling require-

---

[16] An interesting exploration of the predominance of the functional basis of division of labor is provided by Stanley H. Udy, "The Development of Differentiation in Organizational Work," in *Studies in Organization Design,* Jay W. Lorsch and Paul R. Lawrence, eds. (Homewood, Ill.: Irwin, 1970).

ments, costs of new equipment, labor rates, etc. All of this information forms the external environment of the unit. For the managers in the unit such information is the substance from which decisions are fashioned and upon which action is based.

Because the environment of an industrial organization contains a wider range and variety of information and data than a single manager or group of managers can handle, Lawrence and Lorsch argue that industrial organizations tend to become internally segmented into functional units, each of which has the specialized task of dealing with a particular sector of the total environment. Thus, in most industrial organizations, one finds a marketing unit dealing with the market sector of the environment; a manufacturing unit handling, as we have seen, information about process technology and economics (the techno-economic sector); and a research unit dealing with the scientific sector of the external environment.

Lawrence and Lorsch also found that information in each of these three sectors of an industrial organization's external environment tend to have different properties along three dimensions. First, these sectors may differ in the extent to which they confront personnel with *certain* or *uncertain* information. Thus, scientists in a research laboratory usually face more uncertain data than do sales managers in a marketing department. Second, the environmental sectors may vary in the speed with which they provide personnel data about the results of their actions (*time-span of feedback*). For example, managers in manufacturing units often obtain daily or weekly feedback about results, while research scientists may have to wait months or even years for definitive results. Finally, the information in the three sectors may vary in terms of the *dominant strategic issues*. In the market sector the dominant issue is usually meeting customer needs and anticipating competitors' actions, while in the techno-economic sector the focus is on issues of cost and the efficiency of the processing technology.

Lawrence and Lorsch found, not only that different parts of the same environment vary in these characteristics, but also that major variations in these characteristics existed across the three industrial environments they studied (plastics, consumer food products, and standardized containers). This finding is worth bearing in mind when we later discuss the findings of the current study, because it points to the danger of generalizing from the findings about a particular type of functional unit in a particular industry to the same type of unit in another industry. What we must constantly remember is that the important implications in a contingency approach come from understanding the relationships among the environmental variables and the other variables we shall consider, and not from assuming that all functional units with a given name—for example, research or sales—will face the same external environmental characteristics.

With this overview of Lawrence and Lorsch's concept of, and data about, an organization's external environment, it is possible to review their findings about the contingent relationship which exists between these external environmental parameters and internal organizational attributes. They have found that segmenting an organization into functional units leads to a state of *differentiation* within the organization. Essentially, this means that in an effective organization, each unit develops characteristics which enable it to deal with a particular sector of the environment, but which may make it different from other units. Such a state of differentiation is a characteristic of any complex system. To use the human body as an example, the eyes, ears, and nose are differentiated subsystems, which have particular characteristics that enable them to deal with unique environmental stimuli. Of course, inputs from all these subsystems must be integrated through the brain so that the person acts in a coordinated fashion to these diverse sources of data. This fact points to a second major state which any complex system must achieve: *integration*. Lawrence and Lorsch were concerned with how effective organizations achieve both differentiation and integration. In fact, they focused the preponderance of their discussion on how integration or collaboration among differentiated units is achieved. However, for our discussion of the relationship between man and his work organization, we are primarily concerned with their findings about the relationship between unit organizational characteristics and the external environment which results in differentiation among functional units. It should be re-emphasized here that it is within the functional units that the interaction among human task and organizational variables is likely to be most intense.

Lorsch and Lawrence define differentiation in organizations as the *differences in cognitive and emotional orientations among members of different units and the differences in formal structure among units.*[17] Specifically, differentiation was measured along four dimensions:

1. Formality of structure (e.g., high reliance on formal rules, procedures, and tight spans of control vs. the opposite conditions)

[17] Lawrence and Lorsch, *Organization,* p. 6.

2. Goal orientation (concern with market goals vs. concern with cost; quality and efficiency goals vs. concern with scientific goals)
3. Time orientation (long-term vs. short-term goals)
4. Interpersonal orientation (contact with others—concern for getting the job done vs. concern for getting along with others)

Their basic finding was that, in effective organizations, there was generally a match between where a functional unit's organization stood on these dimensions and the nature of its external environment.[18] For example, if the unit in an effective organization faced a highly certain environment (e.g., a production plant), it tended to have a greater formality of structure. On the other hand, where the unit faced a more uncertain external environment (e.g., a research laboratory), there tended to be less formality of structure. Based on these data, they argued that when the information with which a unit must deal is more certain or predictable, the unit will be more effective, placing greater emphasis on formal rules and procedures, tighter spans of control, specific and frequent measures of performance, etc. In an uncertain information field, a unit would be more effective with less formality in its practices and structure.

With regard to the goal orientation of unit members, they found that unit personnel in effective organizations tended to be more oriented toward goals which were consistent with the dominant strategic variables in their part of the environment. For example, in a sales unit within an effective organization facing a market environment, members' goals focused on serving customers, meeting competitive pressures, etc. Members of the manufacturing unit in the same organization were oriented toward cost and efficiency goals, which were appropriate to the external issues they faced. In effective organizations, unit members' time orientation was found to be consistent with the time-span of feedback from the unit's environment. When the unit in such organizations received rapid feedback from its environment, unit members were short-term oriented. In the same organization, members of units receiving less rapid feedback were more long-term oriented.

Finally, based on the work of Fiedler, Lawrence and Lorsch predicted and generally found that, in effective organizations, there was a curvilinear relationship between unit members' interpersonal orientations and the

---

[18] Organizational effectiveness was operationally defined by Lawrence and Lorsch to mean effectiveness in economic terms; that is, growth in profits, sales, and return on investment for the total organization, not in terms of the performance of each functional unit.

TABLE 1-1 Lawrence and Lorsch's
Unit Organization-Environment Fit

Organizational characteristics	Environmental characteristics
Formality of structure	Certainty of information
Interpersonal orientation	Certainty of information
Time orientation	Time-span of feedback
Goal orientation	Dominant strategic variable

certainty of the unit's external environment.[19] When the unit's environment was either highly certain or highly uncertain, members were more oriented to getting the job done as they interacted with each other. Examples of such situations might be a manufacturing or research unit in an effective organization. Where the environment was moderately uncertain, unit members tended to be more oriented toward maintaining interpersonal relationships as they worked together. Such a match was often found in the sales units of effective organizations.

These connections between unit organizational characteristics and environmental properties identified by Lawrence and Lorsch are summarized in Table 1-1. Basically, these authors found that functional units which had such matches between organizational and environmental attributes would be more apt to occur in organizations which achieved favorable total economic results in terms of growth in sales, profits, and return on investment. In the less effective organizations, such congruence was not as prevalent. Thus, the link between this organization-environment fit and functional unit performance was an indirect one. Units which had a better fit with their environment were in organizations achieving more effective *total* economic results (profits, etc.). Based on this evidence, it was asserted that such a fit was likely to be related to more effective performance by each individual functional unit. Such an assumption seems logically sound, not only because the performance of the whole must be dependent upon the performance of the parts, but also because when the unit has a structure and its members have orientations which meet environmental requirements, the members would seem more capable of effectively doing their jobs of processing environmental informa-

[19] Fred E. Fiedler, *A Theory of Leadership Effectiveness* (New York: McGraw-Hill, 1967).

tion, reaching decisions and implementing them. This assertion is also consistent with the experimental results of Leavitt, which showed that small groups were more effective in completing tasks when the communication pattern within the group matched the degree of certainty of their assigned task.[20] Nevertheless, there is as yet no hard evidence that a fit between unit organization and external environment is, in fact, related to more effective *unit performance.* Therefore, as previously mentioned, one of the secondary purposes of the current study has been to establish more solidly whether, in fact, such a link does exist.

Another limitation of the Lawrence and Lorsch findings is that they cover only four internal characteristics of unit organizations. As the authors themselves recognized, this is a very crude map of the more complex territory which exists in any functional unit. Therefore, another secondary goal of our present study has been to broaden the range of the organizational variables covered. Our rationale for selecting particular additional variables will be discussed later; first, it is necessary to relate the Lawrence and Lorsch findings to our primary purpose of including the nature of organization members in the contingency model.

If we accept as a working hypothesis the notion that there is a link between a unit's effectiveness in dealing with its part of the environment and the organization environment fit found by Lawrence and Lorsch, we are still left with the question of why such a relationship exists. One possible explanation, as suggested above, is that when the organization has characteristics fitting the informational field, which composes its external environment, members are able to more effectively process information to reach decisions and act upon them. For example, persons working within a certain environment can be more effective if they have the benefit of clear guidelines from a set of formal procedures and rules. A second possible explanation is that the fit between an organization and its external environment and its relationship to effective unit performance may be connected to what goes on inside the individual member's mind. That is, somehow the complex relationship among organizational characteristics, external environmental forces, and the unit's performance also interacts with the individual member's personality, so that he becomes more enthusiastically committed to his work and produces more effective results. Clearly, these two potential

[20] Harold J. Leavitt, "Some Effects of Certain Communication Patterns on Group Performance," in *Readings in Social Psychology,* Eleanor Maccoby, et al., eds. (New York: Holt, Rinehart & Winston, 1958).

explanations are not mutually exclusive; in fact, they may be closely inter-related. It may be that when the unit organization fits the environment, the individuals are able to act in a way which is consistent with the demands of their jobs and, therefore, they accomplish more and feel better about themselves and their work. These positive feelings may lead them to devote more effort to the work and this reinforces the cycle. It is such a combination of explanations that our study will explore in order to answer the question of how the characteristics of organization members can be included in contingency theory.

The Individual in the Internal Environment

To investigate this, we need to expand the contingency conceptual framework developed by Lawrence and Lorsch to include the characteristics of organization members. Like an organization, an individual can be viewed as a system of interrelated parts which interacts with its environment. Just as various scholars who have viewed organizations as systems have used different variables to describe the internal characteristics of these systems, personality theorists have used a variety of concepts to describe the structure and processes of individual personality systems.[21] In fact, because there has been so much more work done on personality theory, there is a wider variety of theories for describing and explaining the internal functioning of individual personalities than for studying organizations. If our goal was to understand the internal personality functioning of organization members in detail, the wide variety of available personality theories could create a serious problem. However, since our intention is to explore the *relationship* between organization members' characteristics and the other variables in contingency theory, the problems in selecting a formulation about individual personality are not so complex. What is required is a general statement of how we view the individual's personality system and its development and

[21] See, for example, Salvatore R. Maddi, *Personality Theories: A Comparative Analysis* (Homewood, Ill.: Irwin, 1968) for a summary of many of the divergent views of the human personality. While many of these theorists do not explicitly label the personality a system, it seems clear at a general level that many of them treat the internal structure and processes as an interconnected system functioning in an environment of here and now stimuli. Theorists who treat the human personality more explicitly as a system are Karl Menninger, et al., *The Vital Balance* (New York: Viking, 1963); Gordon W. Allport, *Pattern and Growth in Personality* (New York: Holt, Rinehart and Winston, 1937); and Russell L. Ackoff and Fred E. Emery, *On Purposeful Systems* (Chicago: Aldine, 1972).

how this is connected to the way individual systems interact with the organizational system and the work to be done. In developing our position on these issues we have tried to draw upon those aspects of personality systems for which there seems to be broad agreement among personality theorists.[22]

From this perspective, we assume that organization members join organizations with a relatively well-established pattern of tendencies to act in certain ways. This pattern is influenced at the most basic level by their biological makeup, which consists of underlying drives such as those for survival, aggression, affection, mastery. But these basic drives are shaped and defined by a process of social learning from infancy through adulthood.[23] Individuals learn within the family, at play, in school, and at work about what behavior is personally rewarding, and their persistent patterns of behavior in adulthood are a function not only of their biological makeup, but also of this socialization process. This view of personality formation leads to the often-stated conclusions that in some ways all people are the same and in other ways all people are different. The similarities derive from uniformities in biological makeup and in social experience, while the differences are attributable to the unique pattern of biological forces in each of us and the particular life experiences each individual has. We shall be concerned, not only with the similarities among people, but, most importantly, with the way in which members of units with different external environments have different personality predispositions.

Conceiving of these issues in systems terms, we can argue that organization members join an organization with their personalities in an equilibrium state.[24] The particular equilibrium is a function of biological forces and prior socialization, but it is not static. Instead, it is a dynamic balance with a tendency for the system to become both more differentiated or complex and better integrated over a period of time.[25] The "here and now" inputs about what is expected of him that a person receives from the work setting clearly influence how he will act, but the meaning of this feedback will be filtered through the nature of each individual's particular personality balance. Therefore, while Allport has characterized the individual as an open system, it may be more precise to think of the organization member as a

[22] Maddi, *Personality Theories.*
[23] Erik H. Erikson, "The Problems of Ego Identity," in *Identity and Anxiety,* Maurice Stein, et al., eds. (New York: Free Press, 1960).
[24] Allport, *Pattern and Growth.*
[25] Maddi, *Personality Theories,* p. 461.

filtered system.[26] Information is absorbed from the environment, but its meaning is interpreted in a way which is generally consistent with the system's balance, shaped by one's biological makeup and prior life experience.

This general view of the individual organization members as a system will be elaborated in Chapter 3 in terms of the specific individual system characteristics which are the focus of this study. At this point, if we view organization members as systems, we must turn to the question of defining the environment in which these systems operate. So far in this discussion we have used the terms *work setting* or *organization* to define implicitly the individual member's environment at work. To be more explicit about this matter we shall adopt the term *internal environment* to refer to the individual system's environment and to distinguish this from the organizational system's external environment which has been defined previously.[27] The internal environment is defined as the set of signals available to organization members about what is expected of them. These signals are shaped by the formal organizational and measurement practices in the unit and by the expectations of superiors, subordinates, and peers. While we make a conceptual distinction between internal and external environments, it should be recognized that in actuality, organization members may receive data directly from the external environment, as well as from the internal environment. The internal environment is, in a sense, a mediator between the individual and the work he must perform (the external environment). Stated another way, the internal environment is man's explicit and implicit invention to help members relate to the work of the organization in dealing with the external environment. We, therefore, shall explore the relationship between individual systems and both the external environment and the internal environment as it is shown in Fig. 1-1.

Four broad characteristics of the internal environment are of concern in this study. Two of these, goal orientations and time orientations, come directly from the work of Lawrence and Lorsch.[28] Members of a unit are

[26] Allport, *Pattern and Growth*.

[27] The concept of the internal or inner environment has been used in a number of different contexts. For example, see L. J. Henderson, *On the Social System* (Chicago: University of Chicago Press, 1970) p. 153; Herbert Simon, *The Sciences of the Artificial* (Cambridge: MIT Press, 1969) pp. 6-7; Claude Bernard, *An Introduction to the Study of Experimental Medicine* (English translation: New York: Macmillan, 1927); and Charles J. Christenson, "Introduction to Organization and Control" (Boston: Intercollegiate Case Clearing House, 1971).

[28] Lawrence and Lorsch, *Organization*.

Fig. 1-1. A schematic view of systems and environments.

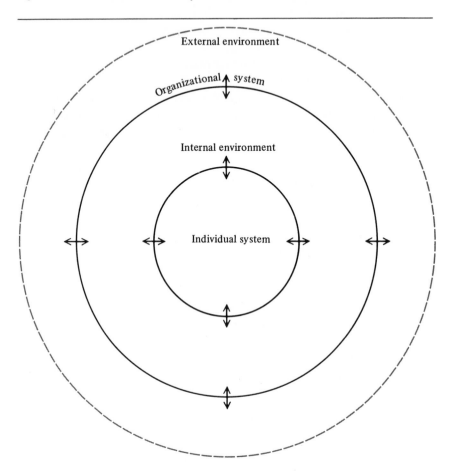

expected to be concerned with a particular set of goals and to be oriented toward a particular time frame. In addition, organization members receive messages about how much influence or control they are expected to have over their own and others' activities. Finally, there is the issue of how closely members are expected to work with others in their unit. To what extent are organization members expected to coordinate their activities with each other? In considering these four issues we shall be dealing with a broader range of variables to describe the internal environment of functional units than Lawrence and Lorsch did; by doing so, we will achieve one of our secondary goals, that of expanding the range of internal variables considered in the contingency approach.

Another secondary goal of this study has been to more carefully investigate the link between effective performance of a functional unit and an external-internal environment fit. As noted above, we would predict from the findings of Lawrence and Lorsch that in effective total organizations there would be a fit between these internal environment characteristics and the nature of the external environment. The time orientation in the internal environment should match the time-span of feedback from the external environment; the goal orientation in the internal environment should be consistent with the dominant strategic issues in the external environment; the degree of autonomy or control in the internal environment should fit the degree of certainty in the external environment; and the degree of coordination of effort among unit members should match the coordination required by the external environment. In addition, we will explore whether such congruence is related *to the performance of each functional unit.*

Based on this way of thinking about the individual-organization relationship, our basic question can now be restated in this fashion: Does a fit among internal environment, external environment, and the individual members' systems relate to effective performance for the unit as well as rewards for the individual? See Fig. 1-2 for a schematic overview of their relationships.

Putting the question in this way emphasizes our view of the relationship between individual and organization as essentially one of exchange.[29] The organization obtains members' efforts toward its goals in return for which members are given, not only economic rewards, but also psychological rewards from their group membership and the work itself.[30] It is with these psychological rewards—specifically, the individual's feelings of competence or mastery from his work—that we shall be particularly concerned.[31] By feelings of competence we mean the extent to which individuals gain psycho-

---

[29] A parallel view is taken by James March and Herbert Simon as organizational theorists, in *Organizations* (New York: John Wiley, 1958) and Harry Levinson as a psychologist in *The Exceptional Executive* (Cambridge: Harvard University Press, 1968).

[30] A. K. Rice, *Productivity and Social Organization: The Ahmedabad Experiment* (London: Tavistock Publications, 1958) and Frederick Herzberg, *Work and the Nature of Man* (Cleveland: World Publishing, 1966).

[31] Robert W. White, "Ego and Reality in Psychoanalytic Theory," *Psychological Issues*, 3 (1963):33.

Fig. 1-2. An overview of the relationships explored.

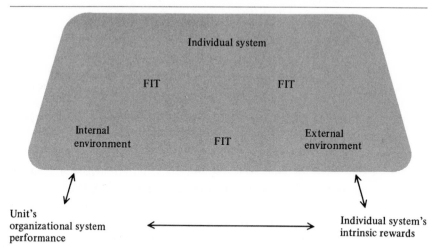

logical gratification from successfully mastering the world around them, including their activities at work.

The sense of competence and the other variables in this conceptual framework have been defined at a general level. In the chapters which follow, we shall elaborate these concepts and describe the measures used to make them operational. In Chapter 2, we will describe the design of the study in order to explore all of these relationships and the measures used to validate our selection of external environments and units for study within these environments. Chapter 3 describes our investigation of the nature of individual members' systems and presents our data about the fit between these characteristics and the nature of the external environment. In Chapters 4 and 5 we will explore the relationship between external and internal environment and how each relates to psychological rewards for the individual and to the performance of the unit. In the final chapter, we will summarize our view of the individual in contingency theory, and expand upon its implication for building and administering organizations.

Before turning to the main body of this discussion, it should be stressed that this conception of the transaction between man and organization has certain limits. For example, it focuses on sense of competence as the only reward for working in an organization. Obviously, other factors such as money, social contact, etc., which we have not explicitly considered, may also be important, not only as indicators of one's competence, but also for their intrinsic value. Also in undertaking a study based on this set of ideas, we are very much aware that we are running the risk of criticism because we are attempting to deal with a wide spectrum of variables. On the one hand, we are concerned with issues familiar to organizational theorists, those of organizational structure, the relationship between organization and environment, etc. On the other, we are concerned with issues of concern to organizational psychologists, for example, the rewards persons gain from work, personality theory, etc. In essence, we have been engaged in building a bridge between these two fields. Such bridge-building is always risky because one is open to criticism from both banks of the stream. Clearly, our conceptualization and methodology may lack the precision to satisfy either the sociologically or psychologically oriented reader. While we are not sanguine about the risks, we feel they are worth taking because our target is to understand the person within an organization in a way which will help the practicing manager. Therefore, it is important to use a model like the one we have just described so that all such variables can be explored simultaneously. This approach addresses the true complexities facing practicing managers by taking into account variations in tasks and organizational conditions, and differences among individuals in the way in which they seek rewards from work. It also provides a picture of the complex system of feedback loops and exchanges which exist between man and organization.

Emphasizing the necessity for developing a theory of organizations which is useful to practicing managers is an appropriate note upon which to conclude this introductory chapter. For our goal throughout this book will be to present our ideas so that they can be understood, not only by theoretically oriented readers, but also by those actively involved in management. Like the problems of straddling psychological and sociological issues, developing a theory which can be of use to practitioners is also a risky endeavor. But here, too, we have no doubts that the risks are worth taking.

2

The study sites
and research design

Criteria for the Selection of Sites

To explore the set of relationships described in Chapter 1, we have selected as research sites several organizational units dealing with relatively certain environments with short-term performance feedback and a relatively high requirement for coordination, and several units dealing with environments characterized by high uncertainty, longer-term performance feedback, and relatively low demands for intraunit coordination. Included among the sites in each type of environment are some highly effective performers and some less successful. Our two major criteria for site selection were (1) the characteristics of the external environment and (2) the performance of the units themselves.

Lawrence and Lorsch, as well as Duncan, have found that manufacturing units of industrial firms generally deal with relatively certain external environments, while research and development laboratories within such firms generally cope with relatively uncertain environments.[1-2] From these findings, we predicted a priori that selecting manufacturing plants and research laboratories as sites for this study would give us a reasonable representation of certain vs. uncertain external environments. We also expected that by selecting such units we would find the contrasts in the time-span of feedback and in the requirements for coordination within the unit that we were seeking. Additionally, we recognized in advance that such units would face environments with very different dominant strategic issues. The relatively certain environment faced by production plants should provide quick feedback about performance, and should require a high degree of members' coordination as well as a strategic focus on costs, schedules, and quality. In contrast, we expected that the relatively uncertain environment with which research laboratories were dealing would typically provide longer-term performance feedback, while requiring less intraunit coordination and a strategic concern with innovation and the development of new knowledge.

Because these environmental parameters are so central to this study, it was necessary to test these a priori assumptions about the environments facing production plants and research laboratories in order to confirm that expected differences in this criterion variable actually did exist. Such an approach is recommended for all social science studies, but it is too seldom followed in field studies of organizations.[3] We, therefore, administered a questionnaire to gauge environmental certainty and time-span of feedback, and we collected clinical interview data from members in each site in order to support the results of the questionnaire and to investigate coordination requirements and strategic concerns.

Ten units were selected for study: four manufacturing plants and six research laboratories. In selecting sites of each type, we obtained five matched pairs of units, each matched pair coming from a different large company. As judged by top management in each of the five companies, one unit in each pair was a highly effective performer and one less effective. Asking these top managers to select pairs of high- and low-performing units

[1] Paul R. Lawrence and Jay W. Lorsch, "Differentiation and Integration in Complex Organizations," *Administrative Science Quarterly* 12 (June 1967):1-47.

[2] Robert B. Duncan, "Characteristics of Organizational Environments and Perceived Environmental Uncertainty," *Administrative Science Quarterly*, 17 (September 1972): 313-327.

[3] Claire Seltzit, et al., *Research Methods in Social Relations*, 3rd ed. (New York: Holt, Rinehart & Winston, 1959).

is admittedly a subjective approach to unit performance evaluation. However, this seemed to be the most practical approach so long as the companies from which the pairs were chosen were all relatively successful in their industry, which in fact they were. The managers in these firms, based on the performance data available to them and their own intimate knowledge of operations, were far more qualified than we to make performance judgments. As we shall make clear later in this chapter, all available objective performance criteria and our interview data with lower-level managers in the sites consistently supported the performance judgments made by the top company managers.

The External Environment of Manufacturing Plants

One pair of plants manufactured standardized containers on high-speed, highly automated, continuous-flow production lines. The other pair, although manufacturing some elements of the final product, primarily assembled already-fabricated components to produce a line of major household appliances.

In the container plants (one located on the East Coast and the other in the Midwest), the finished containers were shipped directly to industrial customers to be used on their own high-speed packing lines. These customers generally selected suppliers on the basis of on-time delivery and product quality. One manager in one of the container plants summarized these strategic issues especially well:

> There's not that much difference in price among our competitors so a customer mainly looks for 99-100 percent efficiency in running our containers. It's got to be a trouble-free product that will run on his automatic lines with a minimum of foul-ups. The difference between 95 percent efficiency and 99 percent efficiency in running our containers on a customer's lines can make or break us with him. And he wants our containers when *his* lines are ready for them, so we break our backs getting them there on time, even when we have just a one-day lead time. That takes a lot of coordination among our people. All of our competitors make a pretty standardized and interchangeable product, and we know that if our deliveries are not on time, the customer will use another supplier whose trucks *have* arrived because he can't shut down his lines and wait for us. This may not hurt us in the short-run because customers usually have to keep a number of suppliers to fill their needs, but if we're late too often it could mean long-term gains for our competitors and losses for us.

Production workers in this industry, for the most part, were unskilled and quickly trained on the job, allowing the plants to augment their regular work force easily during seasonal rushes. The maintenance mechanics who serviced the machinery in the plant, much of which incorporated automated feed-lines, held the highest-skilled jobs in the plant. Two strong national unions represented the workers in these plants and defined a comprehensive set of both local and national rules for the plants.

In the second pair of plants (both located in the Midwest, but not in the same metropolitan area), continuous feed-lines carried components past workers who assembled large-sized appliances. A high level of coordination in work activities was required to ensure that all of the operations were performed. Otherwise, the appliance would generally have to run completely around the assembly cycle again to finish up whatever work was necessary. Separate lines were set up to handle specific categories of appliances, but the operations on each line were easily interchangeable. For example, a man could move from one line to another and not have to change his job classification, duties, or pay scale. The assembled appliances were shipped to the company's own dealers, who then sold them through retail outlets. Company and plant managers generally agreed that the dominant strategic issues for plants in this industry were (1) meeting schedules, (2) maintaining high-quality standards, and (3) meeting and improving cost standards. One plant manager pointed out that these issues all had to be dealt with by operating the assembly line efficiently:

> The most important responsibility we have is to keep the lines running. We've got to keep the lines going, first and foremost. Only then can we worry about solving whatever problem has cropped up. Costs, standards, quality—none of these means a damn unless you see that lines don't shut down.

As in the container plants, workers in the appliance assembly plants were represented in labor negotiations by strong unions which defined pervasive and specific local and national rules. And, as in the container plants, workers in the assembly plants were relatively unskilled and easily trained on the job, with the exception of the skilled mechanics who ensured that the automatic feed-lines kept moving.

Top executives in all four plants and those in the parent companies from which the plants were selected said in interviews that the external environment of each of these plants was relatively certain. For both pairs of plants, the most problematic aspect of the environment was information about scheduling operations to meet customer demand. Such information was somewhat less routine and predictable than information about production methods and technology. In addition, in the appliance plants, the introduction of new models and the necessity of relying on outside suppliers for many vital component parts brought another measure of uncertainty. But once schedule and operations planning had been determined (a daily and/or weekly occurrence in both the container and the appliance plants), the automated nature of plant facilities took over. With the exception of the inevitable rush order that had to be inserted into the plants' schedules and the inevitable delays of appliance components from suppliers, managers in the plant could easily predict and determine the number and the specifications of the product rolling off their lines. In a very real sense, much of the information from these units' environments was defined and built into the automated facilities. One supervisor in one of the container plants explained:

> Once the schedule is made up, and if we can get away with only a few changes in it, we really can just push the "GO" button, sit back, and let the [automated production process] turn out the containers. We know as soon as we come in here in the morning how many containers, what sizes, what labels, etc., have to be run. And if the schedulers let us alone during the day, and if the lines hold up, we surely will get what we're supposed to coming off the line. It's no big mystery making a container like this.

A manager in one of the appliance plants said:

> The speed of the lines in the plant generally determines how many units we produce in any given hour in any given day. Theoretically, we can determine at the start of any shift exactly how many appliances in what categories and styles we'll produce by referring to simple equations that incorporate such things as line speed, learning curves, and line balance. Whatever difficulties we have in any shift more than likely are *not* related to the automated assembling equipment—the most common difficulties are the late suppliers and absent workers.

Just as the environmental information and knowledge required to do these manufacturing tasks well was clear and unambiguous, so the rate of change in that knowledge was slow. A new material for constructing the standardized containers had been developed recently and new and more interchangeable component parts were available for the basic line of appliances, but these were the only major innovations made in the last few years. And, although new types and styles of appliances were always being developed to satisfy consumer tastes, all these developments and innovations required only minimal changes in the basic manufacturing and assembly operations. All were easily incorporated and programmed into the existing technology.

Feedback concerning the effectiveness of performance in the plants was immediate or, as one manager in a container plant put it, ". . . like 15 minutes after the customer uses our container on his lines." Even though the container-manufacturing process involved extremely high-volume operations (an average plant in this segment of the container industry could manufacture 4000–4500 containers each hour), it was usually possible by inspection of the final product to determine the day, the shift, and even the operator responsible for any defect, thereby adding to the degree of certainty. In the appliance plants, normal through-put time [4] for the majority of items was one or two days (line capacities varied from an average of 25 per hour to 70 per hour). Regular inspection points detected defects before the appliance moved to a new station on the line, and a final major inspection occurred at the end of each assembly line. Feedback indicating corrections was necessary in work procedures and the evaluation of component parts was available within minutes of task performance.

As the managers quoted above suggested, coordination of members' work behavior had to be exceptionally high in both pairs of plants. Both relied on continuous-feed production lines whose flow was predetermined by a centralized scheduling group. This group daily received information from customers, from plant supervisors, from inventory planners, etc., and, together with the plant manager scheduled precisely what was to be manufactured and assembled in what sequence. To meet customers' needs, it was important that the schedule be followed religiously by plant employees. Equally important, the schedulers and the plant manager had to know what emergencies made it necessary to deviate from the programmed schedule and when to insert a rush order or to combine similar orders to achieve the cost savings of longer runs. These deviations placed an even higher premium on effective patterns of coordination within the plants. A manager in one of the appliance assembly sites said:

> If people don't work together in this plant, we can't provide the kind of customer service that's the lifeblood of the industry. When I say "work together," I mean not just around the [daily] schedule we get. I mean "work together" around the hundreds of times you have to bend the schedule so that a special request or a really important order can be processed. It's easy to bitch at times like that, and that's when "working together" really is put to the test.

In summary, interviews with managers, coupled with our own observations of plant operations, indicated that all four plants were working in a certain

---

[4] Through-put was the total elapsed time from the beginning of the assembly operations to the time the assembled unit was ready to be stored or shipped.

Fig. 2-1. The certainty and time-span of feedback of the production environments.

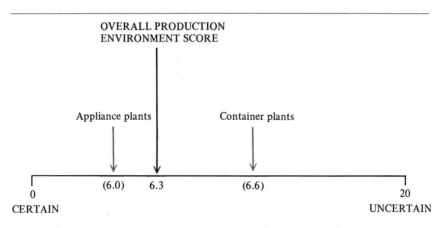

Scores for time-span of feedback and the other two dimensions of certainty used in the study for the two pairs of plants are as follows (the lower the score, the greater the certainty and the shorter the time-span of feedback):

Type of plant	Time-span of feedback of performance	Clarity of information about the task	Programmability of the task	Total score
Container plants (respondents = 9)	1.2	1.7	3.7	6.6
Appliance plants (respondents = 11)	2.0	1.0	3.0	6.0

external environment where performance feedback was rapid, coordination requirements were high, and the strategic concerns centered on cost, quality, and delivery. This conclusion about environmental certainty was confirmed by the results of the questionnaire referred to earlier which was administered to company and top plant executives; this is demonstrated in Fig. 2-1. The results are shown as a mean for each of the two pairs of plants and as an overall mean for all four sites. The questionnaire measured the clarity of information about the environment, the time-span required for feedback about performance, and the programmability of the task of dealing with the environment.[5] It is important to note here that these data also support the managers' comments that feedback from the environment occurred rapidly in all the plants. Admittedly crude as a test of major external

[5] Details about this questionnaire are furnished in the "Methodological Appendix."

environmental variables, this questionnaire nonetheless links well to Duncan's descriptions of the characteristics of manufacturing environments.[6] Further, these findings, when combined with our interview data and observations, do support our a priori judgment that these production units faced a relatively certain environment with short-term feedback. And, as we compare these data with that from the research laboratories, it will be even more evident that these plants faced similar, relatively certain, and short-term environments.

The External Environment of Research Laboratories

The first pair of laboratories (both located in the Southwest) worked on basic and applied research in proprietary drugs; the second pair (both in Northern California) worked on basic and applied research in communications technology; and the third (one on the East Coast, the other in the West) concentrated on research in medical technology. All were financed by a combination of internal company funds and government contracts in varying proportions. The laboratory staffs were composed of those with academic degrees and others with practical experience. The typical laboratory included individuals who had either Ph.D.'s or M.S.'s with or without prior work experience, and B.S.'s with prior experience. The scientific disciplines they represented varied with the kind of research performed. For example, the disciplines represented in the drug laboratories included organic and inorganic chemistry, genetics, crystallography, and cryogenics. Those represented in the communications technology labs ran the gamut of metallurgy, astrophysics, solid-state physics, electrophysics, astronomy, and pure and applied mathematics. All of these researchers and scientists typically worked on individual projects which did not have to be highly coordinated with others, although infrequently small two- or three-man teams were formed to take an interdisciplinary approach to a larger project.

The three pairs of laboratories performed what generally would be considered as industrial research. Although some exploratory research was undertaken, managers and researchers in all the sites recognized that the ultimate aim of their efforts was the development of useful ideas for marketable products or technologies for an operating group. A manager in one

---

[6] Duncan, "Characteristics," pp. 322-324; see especially Tables 4 and 5.

of the medical technology labs stressed this as he summarized his feelings about his job:

> My job is really managing the research and development effort to ensure that my group operates with business goals as well as research goals in mind. Our objective is to make it clear to operating and production people that we're doing work that will help them and will result in meeting company profit targets. We're supposed to generate and "massage" knowledge in this laboratory so that it can be applied to current and future company goals.

A manager in one of the communications technology laboratories emphasized the same outlook:

> We like to say that the kind of work we do involves some fundamental research that points to a direction the company wants to go in and some applied work that still doesn't constrain the creativity of our researchers. All this points to the fact that we're doing industrial research here, that is, we've always got in the back of our mind that what we're working on should eventually . . . be taken over by an operating group and result in a new or improved product or technique. We do research in a number of basic areas . . . in commercial communications media, in communications satellites, in home entertainment products and in the transmission of sound and pictures over vast distances. We've got some keen minds churning for us, but it's got to be productive churning . . . churning to improve or add to the technology and products we're in now.

From these comments it can be concluded that the dominant strategic issue facing these laboratories was to develop new knowledge which could be applied in developing new or improved products and technologies appropriate to the firm's business.

Top executives, governing the six laboratories, described the external environment facing the laboratories as uncertain and rapidly changing. Scientists in all of the groups worked on problems that could be approached in a variety of ways with a number of possible solutions. Information and knowledge necessary to work on the kinds of research problems was ambiguous, open to a variety of interpretations, and was always apt to be superseded by further investigation. This knowledge was also continuously expanding and growing. A scientist in one of the proprietary drug labs said:

> When one of the boys in organic chemistry talks to me about something new he's read in the scientific journals, I never see it the way he does. My background in pharmacology and toxicology puts a different slant on the same set of ideas. It's when we talk about those differences that we both learn something . . . I sometimes wonder what I'd do if we researchers in this lab didn't share information among ourselves. It's simply impossible to keep abreast of

all the changes taking place in our research area on your own. You'd spend all your time reading journals and never get into the lab. Some of the ideas I used in my Ph.D. thesis are considered obsolete today. And I got my degree only a few years ago.

The high rate of change in information about the research task was also evident from a scientist in one of the communications technology groups who commented, "We're using ideas on one of the projects I'm working on now that were right out of science fiction five years ago. I try to get my kid to understand how these ideas were unheard of a few years back, but he watches too much TV to be impressed."

Feedback concerning performance of the laboratories generally was very long term. It was often not for five years or more that ideas for a product or technique made the complete transfer from the laboratory to the manufacturing stage. Within this time frame, though, there were often shorter-term indications of the effectiveness of personal performance in terms of the professional acceptance and acclaim of papers, talks, books, or patent disclosures. However, even this relatively short-term feedback was typically expressed in terms of at least several months. A researcher in one of the drug laboratories commented:

> You can't expect to know how a project is going to turn out here for years in some cases. And, if a guy is looking for data that says he's doing a good job every day, he's in the wrong business in here. We have an award that's given out once a year to the project that made the most impact on our reputation during the year. Most of the recipients of the award have been working on their winner for much longer than a year. Just because a fellow gets the award in one year doesn't mean he hasn't been working on his research for three or four. Take a look at the list of winners since 1965—you'll find some pretty far-out projects there with virtually no overlap with the others. We don't think it's exciting to duplicate somebody else's work. We've all got our own bag.

As this scientist also suggests, a variety of individual projects was important to solve the uncertain technical problems in such an environment. As was indicated above, there was not much need to coordinate or integrate individual projects to attain the laboratories' goals. A researcher typically would not have to coordinate his work activities with other researchers. This is not to say that there was no need for interaction among researchers. In fact, as the manager in the medical product laboratory suggested, researchers in these sites often used colleagues as sounding boards for new ideas. The point we wish to emphasize is that there was not much need for a high level of formal coordination of the researchers' work activities.

Thus, all six research laboratories—although operating in three different industries—were working in uncertain and unpredictable external environments which provided relatively long-term performance feedback, requiring them to to be primarily concerned with innovation and with less emphasis being placed on intraunit coordination. As is shown in Fig. 2-2, the conclusions concerning the uncertainty of the environment and the long-term feedback were supported by the data from the environmental questionnaire. The mean score for each of the pairs of laboratories and the overall mean

Fig. 2-2. The certainty and time-span of feedback of the research environments.

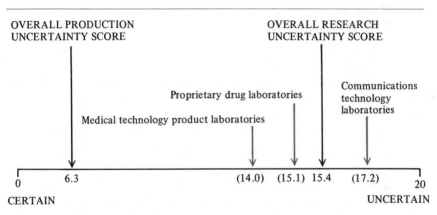

Scores for time-span of feedback and the other two dimensions of certainty for the pairs of laboratories are as follows (the higher the score, the greater the uncertainty and the longer the time-span of feedback):

Type of laboratory	Time-span of feedback of performance [a]	Clarity of information about the task	Programma-bility of the task	Total score
Medical technology products (respondents = 9)	4.7	4.6	4.7	14.0
Proprietary drug laboratories (respondents = 10)	4.5	4.9	5.7	15.1
Communications technology laboratories (respondents = 9)	5.6	5.6	6.0	17.2

[a] These time-span scores can be compared with those for the production plants—1.2 and 2.0 (see Fig. 2-1) to support the generally longer-term feedback confronting the laboratories.

for all six sites are shown. For comparison, we have also plotted the overall mean for the four production plants. These data clearly support the impression that the environments facing the six laboratories were quite similar and much more uncertain than the environments facing the plants. Similarly, the time-span of feedback for the research laboratories was much longer than that for the production plants.

Having examined the environmental characteristics, which were the first set of criteria used to select sites, we now want to examine in more depth the second major criterion used in site selection—the relative performance of these units.

Effective and Less Effective Manufacturing Plants

The two container plants were very much alike in many surface characteristics. As we have seen, they served the same general mix of customers and were subject to the same kinds of market demands for their containers. Physically, the plants were twins. One company executive said, "These two plants are made from the same mold. In fact, the engineers who designed the layout in one did all the work in the other too. You could learn your way around in either one, blindfold yourself, and walk through the other without ever bumping into anything."

The plants were almost identical in age and in number of employees; one plant built in 1952 employed 55 managers and 750–1000 hourly workers, while the other built in 1959 employed 45 managers and 600–850 hourly workers. The same two national unions were represented at both locations, although the managers generally agreed that the unions were somewhat stronger and more demanding at the East Coast site.

The major difference between the two plants was in their relative performance. Top managers evaluated one plant to be a highly effective and successful performer and the other to be much less effective and successful. The return on sales, one of the primary financial criteria in the company's evaluation of its plants, was over eight percent higher in the effective performer. Similarly, the high performer's average production of 5000 containers per hour, another of the primary criteria in the company's evaluation of its plants, ordinarily placed it at or near the top of the company. The less effective performer's average production per hour of 4000 containers placed it well down in the ranks of the company's plants.

The high-performing site was also said to be the top money-making plant in the company.

Both appliance plants were also similar in a number of surface dimensions. The assembly process was the same (although the two plants assembled somewhat different categories and style of appliances, one tending to concentrate on the more expensive ranges and refrigerators and the other on less costly washers and dryers). Both had just under 100 managers and about 1500 hourly workers, and the plants' automated facilities were generally about the same age and state of upkeep.

But these very similar assembly plants had markedly different performance records according to company executives. The costs incurred in the less effective performer tended to be 6-8 percent higher than those for the successful plant. Likewise, the less successful plant typically failed to meet its production schedule by 0.5-1 percent while the effective plant typically beat its schedule by an average of 1-1.5 percent. Concerning the quality of appliances assembled, company managers rated the more effective performer higher than its less successful mate. A top company executive summarized the differences in performance of the two assembly plants:

> The effective performer is as good as our best competitor on its costs, quality, and efficiencies. The other assembly plant has to be rated lower in terms of its performance on costs, efficiencies, and deliveries. The two plants are very similar in what they do, but quite different in how well they do it.

It must be noted that the performance evaluations of top company managers used in the process of selecting our pairs of production plants were never communicated by us to the members of the plants during the study. However, these data seem to indicate that we had selected plants for study which did have different levels of performance.

Effective and Less Effective Research Laboratories

The performance evaluation we used in the research laboratories was based on the judgments of the top managers who were responsible for all the research activity in each company. As in the situation with the production plants, these judgments were made in the process of selecting the laboratory sites and were not communicated to the members of the laboratories. Of course, as we shall explore more fully in later chapters, this is not to say that members of all ten units had not received evaluations of their unit's performance from higher management on previous occasions.

In evaluating laboratory performance, the top managers used some objective criteria such as the number of papers, books, and patent disclosures coming out of the research centers. But their major criterion for evaluation inevitably revolved around the kind of impact the laboratories were making on the operating divisions and on the company goals of growth and profit. This is consistent with the defined task of the laboratories, that is, to do industrial research. Although part of the evaluation of the laboratories' performance rested on how well they interfaced and communicated with operating groups, nonetheless the primary criterion was the utility of ideas developed in the laboratories for transfer to operating sections. Obviously, evaluation of the utility of research ideas is somewhat subjective. Nevertheless, executives seemed to have little trouble distinguishing between the problem-solving effectiveness and creativity of the two laboratories studied in each firm. One top manager in the communications technology company who had executive experience in both laboratories selected from his firm said:

> Our [high-performing] laboratory is doing a magnificent job. It's the best operating division laboratory in the company and some think it's the best in the industry. It has an excellent publication and patent record, but its major plus is that it's doing a great job in serving the engineering groups and production divisions. The other laboratory doesn't appear to be doing as good a job serving its divisions as the first one is. The research coming out of the first one simply has more of a visible impact on the company's goals than does most of the work coming out of the less effective group.

When he was interviewed later in the process of the study, a researcher in the laboratory judged to be the less effective one in the same pair, said:

> We've had trouble here because we spend money to develop things and nothing ever happened with them. It's been pretty difficult to justify some of the things we've done here on the basis of business or profit in the divisions. There are clear indications in the divisions that our research has not had the visible impact on them that they and we would like it to have.

Executives in the proprietary drug company and in the medical technology company saw similar performance differences in their respective pairs of laboratories. An executive in the proprietary drug company, commenting both on the range of problems dealt with in the two laboratories from his company and on the effectiveness of their problem-solving, indicated:

One of the laboratories in the pair has a very broad charter, that is, the researchers there have few constraints concerning the kinds of projects or problems to tackle. In contrast, the other laboratory has a more limited charter in the sense that its job is to focus in on one particular set of problems in proprietary drugs. It's funny, but there is not as much coming out of the former in terms of products or techniques the company can sell or license as there is coming out of the latter, even with its more limiting charter. There's less output in the former in terms of the investment we put in there—less than you'd expect, and they've got a very broad charter that allows them to go pretty much where they want. Given their broad objectives, there are not as many new and useful ideas coming out of that laboratory as there are out of the other with its tighter objectives. The latter group always seems to be coming up with more and more creative ideas—more than one would expect with its limited charter. They're always asking for more and more resources for these new and creative ideas.

When asked what specific criteria were used by the medical products company to evaluate the performance of all its laboratories, one top company executive incorporated into his response an evaluation of the two sites within his company:

Company managers use three criteria to judge the performance of research groups. First, it's the products transferred out and the effect of these products on the profit and growth of the company. Second, it's how well people in the operating and manufacturing groups feel that the laboratory is helping them. And, finally, it's in terms of how good company executives and operating managers feel about the head of the lab. On all three criteria, one of the labs in the pair from our company rates $A+$. That lab does more work for divisions than any other in the company. There is a strong coupling of the lab with the divisions it helps. The other research group doesn't fare as well on these criteria. There are some real problems of effective coupling of that laboratory with operating groups. It hasn't worked out nearly as well as it has in the first group. In terms of the creativity the two groups show in solving problems, the first group again rates an $A+$. It's a highly creative laboratory that is making meaningful contributions to the growth of the company. The other group is less creative and a less high performer.

Based on consistent comments such as these from executives in all three firms, we felt safe in accepting their relatively subjective appraisal of laboratory performance. While more objective criteria such as those used in evaluating the production plants would undoubtedly have been desirable, none existed. Therefore, we have relied on the best available assessment of performance to label one unit in each pair as a high performer and the other as low.

Table 2-1 summarizes our research design, highlighting the two sets of criterion variables we used for the selection of our sites.

TABLE 2-1 Research Design: Characteristics of the External Environment

	Certain: Short-term: high intraunit coordination: manufacturing issues.		Uncertain: Long-term: low intraunit coordination: research issues.		
	Company 1	Company 2	Company 3	Company 4	Company 5
HIGH	Container plant 1[a]	Appliance plant 2[a]	Communications laboratory 3[a]	Drug laboratory 4[a]	Medical technology laboratory 5[a]
LOW	Container plant 1[b]	Appliance plant 2[b]	Communications laboratory 3[b]	Drug laboratory 4[b]	Medical technology laboratory 5[b]

[a] Indicates high-performance units.
[b] Indicates low-performance units.

Research Methods

The data for the study were collected in the ten sites by questionnaires and interviews. As we have seen, data to describe the external environments were gathered from the top executive in each unit and from their superiors in the five large companies who also provided the evaluation of the units' relative performance. Data about members' individual attributes were collected from tests and questionnaires given to a cross section of thirty to forty-five managers and professionals in each of the ten organizational units, as well as from hour-long, open-ended interviews conducted with about half the managers and professionals. Those participating in the study represented different hierarchical levels and performed different functions. For example, managers in the production plants associated with a cross section of functions at all organization levels (down through first-line supervisors) answered the questionnaire and were interviewed. In the research labs, a cross section of the professional staff and management provided these data. In all sites, over one-half of the total group of managers and professionals made up our samples.

Data concerning the internal environments of these units came from several sources. Data about the formal structure of the units, used as one measure of the degree of organizational control in the unit, came from individual hour-long interviews with top unit managers (i.e., laboratory heads in the research units and plant managers in the production units), and from our own first-hand investigation of formal documents and manuals. The findings concerning members' perceptions of the internal environment were collected by questionnaires and interviews with the same employees who provided data about individual attributes.[7] Clearly such perceptual measures are open to criticism as being subject to a *halo effect* which could cause persons in a high-performance situation to rate many of these measures positively simply because they were performing effectively. While we recognized in advance that such criticism could be made of our methodology, we have chosen it for several reasons. First, the particular configuration of variables which we predicted were related to effective performance in the two different external environments were quite different and highly complex; thus, they would be difficult to attribute to a halo effect. Second, the perceptual measures would be supported by interviews

---

[7] Detailed information about our research methods can be found in the "Methodological Appendix."

in each organization, which would provide concrete examples of feelings, perceptions, and expectations in each setting. Third, there appeared to be no alternative method of data collection which would allow testing our theories and predictions within the constraints posed by time and the conditions of entry into these sites.

The statistical treatment of the data also deserves mention. Because this survey is concerned with the overall pattern of variables, we did not conduct intensive tests of statistical correlation of any particular variable with any other. We believed that the overall pattern of relationships among the external environment, members' characteristics, and the internal environment was more important than a statistical test of any one variable against another. The keystone of this study is the contingent relationship among all these variables. However, because our research design was based on matched pairs, we have relied on extensive statistical analyses to establish that statistically significant differences in individual attributes and in specific measures of the internal organization environments did exist between units with different performance levels in both types of environment. It should also be noted that, although we ourselves were aware of differences in performance levels in the matched pairs, those who processed, coded, and scored the questionnaires were unaware of such differences.

Finally, it is important to reemphasize the exploratory nature of this study. Our research design and methods may seem crude to some. However, we are convinced that these issues and problems are important and worthy of exploration. This in itself justifies our having undertaken this study whatever methodological limitations others may see in it.

3

Organization members and the external environment

Initially, we will examine the characteristics of members within the units studied to determine how well these matched the requirements of the unit's external environment. As mentioned in Chapter 1, psychologists have long recognized that in some respects all persons are similar while in other respects all persons are different. The following discussion emphasizes the differences between the members of units working in different external environments having varying performance results. At the outset, however, it is important to discuss what appears to be a common characteristic of all the individuals in this study—a desire to master their surroundings.

Job Mastery and a Sense of Competence

Many researchers have conducted experiments in which they observed a tendency in animals and children to explore and master their external environments. Berlyne, Montgomery, and Harlow, among others, studied animal behavior and concluded that the activity of manipulating and exploring an environment was engaged in because it was satisfying in its own right.[1-3] Similarly, Piaget and Stott provide excellent accounts of exploratory and environmental mastery activities in children.[4-5] They, too, concluded that their subjects engaged in these activities because they were intrinsically pleasurable.

Robert White found in such empirical evidence the basis for proposing that there is a basic, even biological, source of energy in all individuals which enables them to influence and master their external environments. He calls this energy *effectance,* defining it as "inherent in the mental apparatus," and as the active tendency for individuals to behave in such a manner as to influence or master their external environment for its own sake.[6] White terms this subjective feeling of satisfaction that accompanies the use of the effectance energy in influencing individuals' particular environments "a feeling of efficacy." He also indicates that feelings of efficacy have biological roots that are as fundamental as the gratification derived from feeding.[7] The major significance of effectance and a feeling of efficacy for individuals is in the development of their "competence." White describes competence as "a person's existing capacity to interact effectively with his environment" and as "the cumulative result of the whole history of transactions with the environment. . . ."[8] He continues, a "sense of competence describes the subjective side of one's actual competence."[9] In other words, a sense of competence encompasses the subjective feelings which individuals have about their abilities. It reflects their confidence in their own competence, resulting from cumulative interactions with all aspects of their external environment, including work ac-

---

[1] D. E. Berlyne, "Novelty and Curiosity as Determinants of Exploratory Behavior," *The British Journal of Psychology* 41 (1950):68-80.

[2] K. C. Montgomery, "The Role of the Exploratory Drive in Learning," *Journal of Comparative and Physiological Psychology* 47 (1954): 60-64.

[3] Harry F. Harlow, "Motivation as a Factor in the Acquisition of New Responses," *Current Theory and Research in Motivation* (Lincoln, Neb.: University of Nebraska Press, 1953), pp. 24-47.

[4] Jean Piaget, *The Construction of Reality in the Child* (New York: Basic Books, 1954).

[5] D. H. Stott, "An Empirical Approach to Motivation Based on the Behavior of a Young Child," *The Journal of Child Psychological Psychiatry* 2 (1961):97-117.

[6] Robert W. White, "Ego and Reality in Psycholanalytic Theory," *Psychological Issues* 3 (1963):33.

[7] White, "Ego," p. 35.

[8] White, "Ego," p. 39.

[9] White, "Ego," p. 39.

tivities, over their life experience. Just as competence is the cumulative result of the whole history of people's dealings with their environment, so a sense of competence is the cumulative internal set of feelings of confidence about their competence that individuals seek and derive from repeatedly and successfully mastering their environment.

Drawing on White's theoretical formulation, we prefer to use the terms *sense of competence* and *feelings of competence* interchangeably to refer to people's confidence in their own competence. Likewise, following White, we view an individual's sense of competence as the cumulative result of a basic, even biological, energy to explore and master the world around him with which individuals are born. This is shaped and modified over one's life, both by learning from significant others and from dealing effectively with objects in the external world. One's career at school and work plays an important role in this development, although experience in these settings builds upon the learning in the family setting in the person's earliest years. It is important to note that we are not referring to how competent organizational unit members actually are, but rather to their internal feelings about how competent they seem to themselves. These feelings, because they are gratifying to the individual, provide continued incentives to act competently.[10] This feedback from the environment about one's having acted competently enhances one's feelings of competence and induces one to continue one's mastering of the external world. For employed persons, such as the managers and professionals in this study, an important source of feedback about their competence comes from their activities while at work in organizations. How much feedback organization members gain about their competence at work can have an important impact on their feelings of competence.[11]

Members' Sense of Competence Within Manufacturing Environments

Based on these formulations we expected the members of high-performing manufacturing units to feel generally more competent than their counterparts in the lower-performing units. To test this prediction we used two different instruments. One was a projective test which presented the

[10] Robert W. White, "Competence and the Growth of Personality," *Science and Psychoanalysis*, 11 (1967):42-58.

[11] Robert W. White, personal communication, 1972.

respondents with an ambiguous set of pictures of people at work. The respondents were then asked to write brief descriptions about what was going on in each situation. The second technique required the respondents to write a short description of what their day at work would be like on the next working day. These descriptions and stories were then scored for a number of themes which are related to one's sense of competence. (These

Fig. 3-1. Differences in members' sense of competence in the manufacturing plants: The first test (ambiguous pictures).[a]

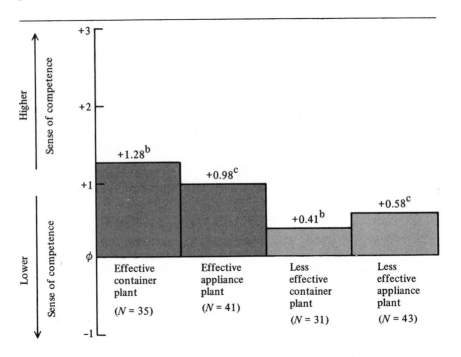

[a] All picture sets used to measure feelings of competence were scored and re-scored by independent scorers. Scores reported are the means for each plant.

[b] The coefficient of correlation (r) between first score and rescore in the container plants was 0.903. The percentage of imagery agreement between first score and re-score was 91.6 percent. The statistical significance of difference in means: one-tailed probability, $t=3.84$; $p=<0.001$.

[c] The coefficient of correlation between first score and rescore in the appliance plants was 0.822. The percentage of imagery agreement between first score and re-score was 84.5 percent. The statistical significance of difference in means: one-tailed probability, $t=2.76$; $p=<.01$.

Fig. 3-2. Differences in members' sense of competence in the manufacturing plants: The second test ("tomorrow's day").[a]

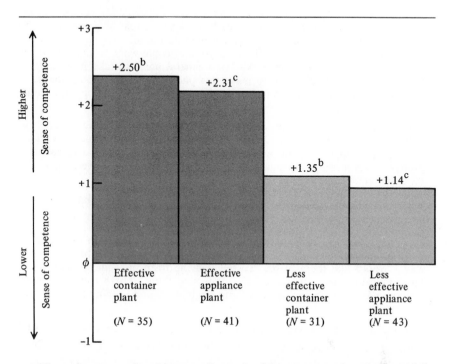

[a] All stories concerning "tomorrow" on the job were scored and rescored by independent scorers. Scores reported are the means for each plant.

[b] The coefficient of correlation (r) between first score and rescore in the container plants was 0.882. The percentage of imagery agreement between first score and rescore was 89.8 percent. The statistical significance of difference in means: one-tailed probability, $t = 3.97$; $p = < 0.01$.

[c] The coefficient of correlation between first score and rescore in the appliance plants was 0.871. Percentage of imagery agreement between first score and rescore was 90.3 percent. The statistical significance of difference in means: one-tailed probability, $t = 2.85$; $p = < 0.01$.

themes, as well as more details on the instruments and scoring techniques, are provided in the "Methodological Appendix.")

The data from both instruments, seen in Figs. 3-1 and 3-2, supported our prediction. The members of the higher-performing plants had significantly greater feelings of competence than did their counterparts in the less effective plants. The following statements which are representative of the feelings expressed by members of the successful plants in the open-ended interviews provide a richer perspective on these quantitative results:

> If a guy wants only a paycheck out of his job, he'll work for you on payday only and not at all times during the week. But we see that he gets pride in his work. It's the best thing you can give a man on the job . . . and you don't find that he'll work for you only on payday. People want to do a good job here. They care about their work. It's a general norm to take pride in your work here. The people want to make this plant the best in the company, so they work every day to keep it on top. We hear we're the best plant around. That's a good feeling. But we're still trying to be better.

> People want to get their jobs done well in this plant. We have a bunch of able, competent individuals. There's a lot of satisfaction for me in working with these people . . . my major frustration is when I think I've solved a problem and it crops up again. I like problems to stay solved once I've tackled them.

The feelings of many managers in the less successful plants seemed especially well expressed by a foreman in the less effective container plant:

> I can't say that I'm really satisfied by the way we do our job in this plant. I don't have many really good days when I feel that operations have been the way I would like them to be. To tell you the truth, nowadays when I just hit standard in production I feel I've done something. There aren't too many of those days though. Some days I run my butt off and nothing happens. It's frustrating.

These clinical data seem to support the view that differences in members' feelings of competence were related to their mastery of their work. Where people worked effectively, they seemed to experience a feeling of competence which motivated them to work harder in the future. However, as we shall discover below, this is only one of several possible explanations for these findings.

Members' Sense of Competence Within Research Laboratories

We also expected that the managers and professionals working in high-performing research laboratories would have greater feelings of competence than would persons working in the less successful laboratories. As is shown in Figs. 3-3 and 3-4, this is precisely what we found on both measures of members' sense of competence. Members of high- and low-performing laboratories made statements which breathe life into the quantitative scores and which support again the idea that feelings of competence were related to effective mastery of the work itself. Members of high-performing labs said, for example:

Fig. 3-3. Differences in members' sense of competence in the research laboratories: The first test (ambiguous pictures).[a]

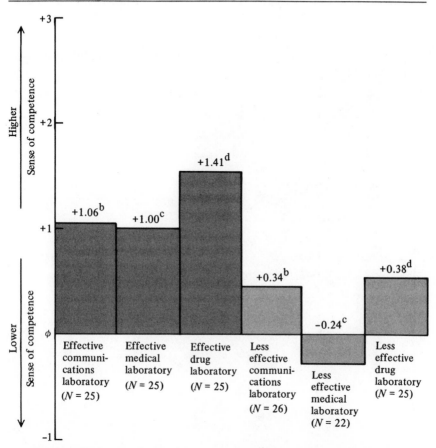

[a] All picture sets were scored and rescored by independent scorers. Scores reported are the means for each laboratory.

[b] The coefficient of correlation (r) between first score and rescore in the communications laboratories was 0.856. The percentage of imagery agreement between first score and rescore was 90.7 percent. The statistical significance of difference in means: one-tailed probability, $t=2.83$; $p=<0.01$.

[c] The coefficient of correlation (r) between first score and rescore in the medical products laboratories was 0.767. Percentage of imagery agreement between first score and rescore was 83.4 percent. The statistical significance of difference in means: one-tailed probability, $t=3.74$; $p=<0.001$.

[d] The coefficient of correlation (r) between first score and rescore in the proprietary drugs laboratories was 0.806. Percentage of imagery agreement between first score and rescore was 82.2 percent. The statistical significance of difference in means: one-tailed probability, $t=4.53$; $p=<0.001$.

Fig. 3-4. Differences in members' sense of competence in the research laboratories: The second test ("tomorrow's day").[a]

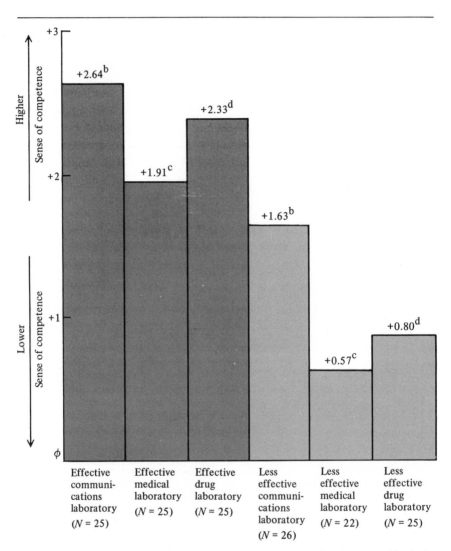

[a] All stories concerning "tomorrow" on the job were scored and rescored by independent scorers. Scores reported are the means for each laboratory.

[b] The coefficient of correlation (r) between first score and rescore in the communications laboratories was 0.877. The percentage of imagery agreement between first score and rescore was 92.4 percent. The statistical significance of difference in means : one-tailed probability, $t=2.71$; $p=<0.01$.

In the past few years, when we wrote a proposal for a contract, we've been almost certain to get it because of our skills and results. We can just about select the kinds of contracts that are especially interesting to us and we're virtually sure to get it. People feel good about that in here—they recognize that they're judged to be the cream of the crop. People here are really doing a good job. People like to come in to their offices here. There's a definite feeling that days are meaningful and profitable.

My biggest kick comes from successfully completing a project. It's great to know you've got a winner. I would say that's the way it usually is too. We've solved a lot of problems here that were bastards when we started on them. You find that, over time, that kind of experience builds up in a research group like this, and it leads to a positive attitude that you couldn't buy for all the money in the world.

Their counterparts in less effective research laboratories reported:

Work hasn't been going very well in our lab. Projects aren't very stimulating. We're not winning too many outside or inside contracts. It finally gets to you as an individual. You've been trained in your scientific area so long that you feel lousy when you can't use your knowledge to help the lab make out. This is a pretty gloomy lab to work in.

We don't feel our skills are being put to the best use in this laboratory. I spent years building up my background and reputation, but now I'm stymied. Not much is going on in here that's exciting any more. The guy who services my car probably has a better attitude concerning his work than I have.

A researcher can make a dollar anywhere. But he's got to have fun too or he gets stale. Some of that fun is gone here. Lots of the researchers aren't having fun any more. It's frustrating. At one time, the company felt that we scientists were so happy with the work we were doing that they didn't have to pay much attention to wages or fringe benefits, etc. Now that the researchers aren't having fun, they tend to be more conscious of their salary and the other tangible things the company can offer. *When you don't get your kicks from your work, you have to get them from your salary or your vacation or your family.* That sums up the attitude of a number of researchers here.

---

[c] The coefficient of correlation (r) between first score and rescore in medical products laboratories was 0.845. Percentage of imagery agreement between first score and rescore was 89.0 percent. The statistical significance of difference in means: one-tailed probability, $t = 2.48$; $p = < 0.02$.

[d] The coefficient of correlation (r) between first score and rescore in the proprietary drugs laboratories was 0.842. Percentage of imagery agreement between first score and rescore was 84.9 percent. The statistical significance of difference in means: one-tailed probability, $t = 3.06$; $p = < 0.01$.

Differences in Members' Sense of Competence: Summary and Three Alternative Explanations

Data summarizing differences in members' feelings of competence, as these relate to the two major criterion variables used for the selection of sites, appear in Table 3-1. In both types of environments, members working in units which were successful felt a higher sense of competence than did members working in units that were less successful. This suggests that while all persons wish to master their environment, there are varying degrees to which members of different units achieve this important source of gratification.

There are at least three possible explanations of why members in high-performing units within both environments felt more competent than those in the lower-performing sites. First, people with an already high sense of competence may have chosen to join the high-performing units or have been chosen for such jobs. Accordingly, effective units simply attract people who have strong feelings of competence before their employment. A second possible explanation, to which we have previously alluded, is that high unit performance may have provided members with feedback that enhanced their feelings of competence. In this view, people are information processors whose patterns of mental activities, such as expectations and feelings, are formed and reformed by information-processing and feedback.[12] In other words, the structure of feelings about competency is the result of the continual processing and reformulation of feedback about performance in the external environment. A third possible

TABLE 3-1 Differences in Members' Feelings of Competence

Manufacturing environment		Research environment	
High performing	Low performing	High performing	Low performing
Significantly higher feelings of competence for members in both sites.	Significantly lower feelings of competence for members in both sites.	Significantly higher feelings of competence for members in all three sites.	Significantly lower feelings of competence for members in all three sites.

[12] Robert R. Holt, ed. *Motives and Thought: Psychoanalytic Essays in Honor of David Rapaport, Psychological Issues,* Monograph 18/19 (New York: International Universities Press, 1967).

explanation is that members of the units in the two separate environments differed in their personality predispositions, so that members of high-performing units in each environment had personality predispositions and behavioral tendencies that better suited the nature of the external environment they were trying to master. In other words, members of high-performing units might have predispositions that were congruent with the external environment.

All three of these explanations seem plausible. Although we have no data to support the idea that effective units attract people with an already strong sense of competence, the explanation seems reasonable and can be supported from plain common sense and anecdotal evidence. Many of the interview comments presented above do support the second possibility—that high unit performance provides information and feedback which, in turn, enhance people's feelings of competence. White recognizes the self-reinforcing aspects of a sense of competence and indicates that seeking feelings of competence is a continual process of feedback.[13] Such a view is also consistent with the work of Hackman and Lawler who point out that attaining an outcome or reward which an individual values can be seen as both a result of (rather than a determinant of) effective performance and an incentive for continual efforts to perform effectively.[14] Argyris, when speaking of individuals experiencing psychological success on the job, seems to hold a similar view.[15] For him, the psychic energy that enables an individual to perform effectively is dependent upon the degree of psychological success or self-esteem that he obtains from his past performance.

The third explanation, that a consistency between people's personality predispositions and the nature of the external environment which shapes their work can lead to high feelings of competence, bears further investigation. White indicates although effectance energy will always be geared toward exploration, novelty, and autonomy in an environment external to the individual, that nonetheless these terms can come to have very different meanings in the service of producing realistic results for adults with different personality predispositions.[16] From this premise we predicted that

[13] White, "Competence."

[14] J. Richard Hackman and Edward E. Lawler, III, "Employee Reactions to Job Characteristics," *Journal of Applied Psychology, Monograph* 55 (June 1971):259-86.

[15] Chris Argyris, *Integrating the Individual and the Organization* (New York: Wiley, 1964).

[16] Robert W. White, "Motivation Reconsidered: The Concept of Competence," *Psychological Review*, 66 (1959):297-333.

different adults would feel competent in mastering different external environments because of differences in their personality makeup. It is now time to consider whether our data support this prediction without rejecting the first two explanations of our findings about the relationship between unit performance and sense of competence. Rather, we believe that there is sufficient anecdotal and prior research evidence to suggest that the first two explanations have some validity. If we can establish the validity of this third possibility, which might be labeled the *fit* explanation, we will then have a clearer view of how the individual interacts with his organizational setting and his work.

In determining whether a strong sense of competence is related to a fit between external environmental requirements and people's personality predispositions, we were faced with a serious problem since psychologists have identified a multitude of personality variables which could be utilized. Rather than attempting to develop a comprehensive profile of the organization members' personalities, we approached the problem by identifying four personality dimensions which we expected would differ because of the variations in external environments described in Chapter 2. Table 3-2 summarizes these characteristics.

The first of these personality dimensions deals with the cognitive structure of members. We are building on the work of Schroder and his colleagues, who found that individuals vary in the extent to which they are able to take in differentiated bits of information from the environment and then to integrate the differentiated bits. This capacity they call

TABLE 3-2 Summary of External Environmental Characteristics and Their Impact on Unit Members

Manufacturing environment	Research environment
Provides rapid, clear, objective performance feedback	Provides infrequent and often ambiguous performance feedback
Presents well-defined work and procedures	Presents few constraints as to how work should be done
Presents simpler and more stable problems	Presents complex and changing problems
Presents work which requires high coordination of effort	Provides work which can be done relatively independently of other projects in the unit

Fig. 3-5. Schematic representation of integrative complexity.

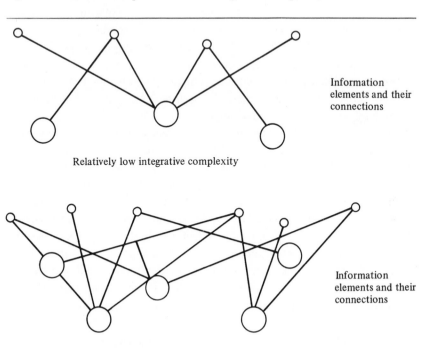

Information
elements and their
connections

Relatively low integrative complexity

Information
elements and their
connections

Relatively high integrative complexity

integrative complexity.[17] Two identifiable aspects of this information processing are (1) the number of dimensions or attributes that individuals differentiate and, (2) the complexity or degrees of freedom individuals use to combine the differentiated dimensions. If an individual differentiates only relatively few elements in his environment and then combines them in relatively fixed and predetermined ways, he is said to be processing information at a low level of integrative complexity. If, on the other hand, he perceives many elements and then integrates them in many intricate ways, he is processing information at a high level of integrative complexity.[18] Figure 3-5 is a schematic representation of integrative complexity.

Following our contingency expectation, we predicted that the individuals

[17] Harold M. Schroder, et al., *Human Information Processing* (New York: Holt, Rinehart & Winston, 1967).
[18] Schroder, et al., *Human,* pp. 14-16, 20.

dealing with complex problems, such as those typical of an uncertain environment, would need a high integrative complexity to have strong feelings of competence, while those dealing with less complex problems in a relatively certain environment would have a relatively low integrative complexity related to strong feelings of competence.

The second personality dimension we investigated is members' *tolerance for ambiguity;* that is, preferences for well-defined, stable, and relatively unchanging conditions vs. the opposite conditions. We expected that persons working with an uncertain environment would have a greater tolerance for ambiguity than would those dealing with more certain information and well-defined work. This is so simply because less defined work and greater uncertainty of information would produce a higher level of ambiguity with which the individual must cope. A person's tolerance for ambiguity also would be related to the rapidity with which feedback is obtainable from the environment. When feedback is frequent, persons would not require as high a tolerance for ambiguity as when feedback takes longer. If a match was achieved between the level of an individual's tolerance for ambiguity and these environmental factors, we predicted the individual would be more likely to feel competent than if such a fit were nonexistent.

Persons feeling competent in different external environmental settings might also vary in their *preferred ways of relating to authority*. Individuals dealing with an uncertain external environment, who had more direct influence over defining work roles and providing their own direction, would feel more competent if they preferred more autonomy and did not require strong relationships with authority figures. Persons working with a more certain external environment where many objective performance standards and directions were present would be more likely to feel competent if they felt comfortable with more dependent authority relationships.

Finally, people might differ on what we called *attitude toward individualism* (does a person prefer to work and be alone or in groups?) depending on the nature of the external environment. In environments where little interdependence among unit members was required, persons who preferred being and working alone might feel more competent. On the other hand, persons who preferred spending time with others would tend to feel more competent dealing with external environments which required more coordination among members.

We have labeled these predicted differences as *personality predispositions* because we conceive of them as characteristic tendencies to think, act, and be oriented in certain ways which stem from members' personality development and which will affect their capacity to achieve feelings of competence in a particular external environmental setting. It should be stressed that our selection of these particular dimensions does not indicate that there are not other characteristics along which the personnel in the two types of environments might be similar or different. Rather, these particular characteristics were selected because they seemed especially salient for understanding personality differences, given our advanced knowledge of the kinds of external environments under investigation.

Our expectations concerning the fit between requirements of the external environment and members' personality predispositions leading to strong feelings of competence are summarized in Table 3-3, which also incorporates the findings from Table 3-1, showing actual differences in members' feelings of competence as related to both environmental attributes and the sites' level of performance. We expected that members of high-performing sites, more so than members in low-performing sites, would have personality dimensions well suited to external environmental requirements and that it was this fit which would relate to a strong sense of competence. Accordingly, we must supply the missing data from Table 3-3 to see if our prediction is correct.

In both pairs of manufacturing plants, members in the high- and low-performing sites were *not* very different in any of the four personality predispositions. In fact, members in high- and low-performing sites in both pairs of plants were strikingly similar, as is seen in Table 3-4.[19] As shown by Table 3-5, in all three pairs of research laboratories, members in high- and low-performing sites were again *not* very different in any of the four dimensions.

---

[19] The methodology used to measure the level of integrative complexity of the cognitive structures of the individuals in the survey relied on the analysis of stories written by the respondents. The stories, used initially to score for feelings of competence, lent themselves readily to assessment of the conceptual level of the written responses. To gauge the integrative complexity of the stories, we used scorers who had no involvement in the initial scoring for feelings of competence. The "Methodological Appendix" gives more details about the mechanisms of scoring for integrative complexity. The questionnaire we devised to measure tolerance for ambiguity and attitudes toward authority and individualism is described in full in the "Methodological Appendix." The reliability of the instrument was assessed by computing the Kuder-Richardson reliability coefficient. The obtained reliability was 0.853 on the tolerance for ambiguity segment of the instrument, 0.891 on the attitude toward authority segment, and 0.876 on the attitude toward individualism segment.

TABLE 3-3 The Fit of Environmental Requirements and Members' Personality Dimensions

	Manufacturing environment		Research environment	
	Expectations	Data	Expectations	Data
High performing	Low integrative complexity		High integrative complexity	
	Low tolerance for ambiguity		High tolerance for ambiguity	
	Low attitude toward authority [a]		High attitude toward authority [a]	
	Low attitude toward individualism [a]		High attitude toward individualism [a]	
	High sense of competence	High	High sense of competence	High
Low performing	High integrative complexity		Low integrative complexity	
	High tolerance for ambiguity		Low tolerance for ambiguity	
	High attitude toward authority [a]		Low attitude toward authority [a]	
	High attitude toward individualism [a]		Low attitude toward individualism [a]	
	Low sense of competence	Low	Low sense of competence	Low

[a] The lower the attitude toward authority, the more members are not uncomfortable in strong, controlling authority settings; the higher the attitude toward authority, the more members prefer autonomy and independence in authority relations. The lower the attitude toward individualism, the more members prefer to be and work in groups; the higher the attitude toward individualism, the more members prefer to be and work alone.

It is only when we contrast members operating in the manufacturing external environment with members operating in the research external environment that we discover significant differences, as is demonstrated in Fig. 3-6. Persons working with the research environment scored significantly higher on the index of integrative complexity than did members in the stable production settings. The higher integrative complexity of the members in the uncertain research environment meant that they preferred

TABLE 3-4 Similarities in Personality Dimensions of Members in High- and Low-performing Sites in the Manufacturing Environment [a]

Type of plant	Performance	
Container manufacturing plants	High performer	Low performer
Integrative complexity	4.22	4.25
Tolerance for ambiguity	2.57	2.59
Attitude toward authority	2.15	2.10
Attitude toward individualism	2.45	2.40
Appliance assembly plants	High performer	Low performer
Integrative complexity	4.15	4.19
Tolerance for ambiguity	2.65	2.52
Attitude toward authority	2.23	2.20
Attitude toward individualism	2.38	2.39

	All high-performing sites	All low-performing sites	Overall mean
Integrative complexity	4.17	4.21	4.19
Tolerance for ambiguity	2.63	2.53	2.57
Attitude toward authority	2.20	2.14	2.17
Attitude toward individualism	2.40	2.39	2.40

[a] The differences in means between high- and low-performing sites were *not* significant at the 0.1 level for any of the four dimensions. The N for integrative complexity: all high-performing sites, $N = 76$; all low performing sites, $N = 74$. The N for all other dimensions: all high-performing sites, $N = 73$; all low-performing sites, $N = 70$.

to use many alternative schemes for interpreting external events, that they needed few rules for sensing and responding to environmental information, and that they tended to rely heavily on internal intellectual processes for making sense out of this information. The lower integrative complexity of members working within routine, stable environments signified a preference for adhering to externally imposed fixed rules for processing information, and indicated the sensing of fewer choices or alternatives in working on their tasks.[20]

The researchers working with an uncertain and longer-term external environment also had a significantly higher tolerance for ambiguity, preferred significantly more autonomy in their attitudes toward authority, and

[20] Schroder, et al., *Human,* pp. 16-17, 21-23.

Fig. 3-6. Differences in personality dimensions.

Integrative complexity [a]

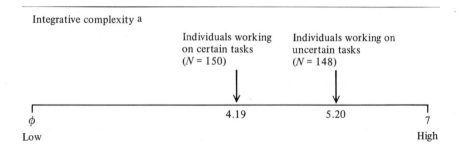

| Individuals working on certain tasks (N = 150) | Individuals working on uncertain tasks (N = 148) |

φ   4.19   5.20   7
Low   High

Tolerance for ambiguity [b]

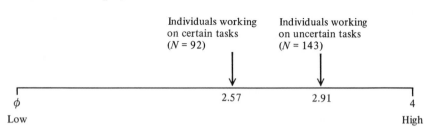

| Individuals working on certain tasks (N = 92) | Individuals working on uncertain tasks (N = 143) |

φ   2.57   2.91   4
Low   High

Attitude toward authority [c]

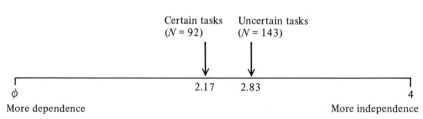

| Certain tasks (N = 92) | Uncertain tasks (N = 143) |

φ   2.17   2.83   4
More dependence   More independence

Attitude toward others [d]

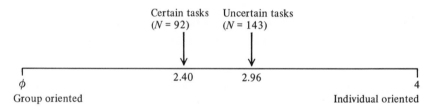

| Certain tasks (N = 92) | Uncertain tasks (N = 143) |

φ   2.40   2.96   4
Group oriented   Individual oriented

---

[a] All tests were scored and rescored for integrative complexity by independent scorers. The overall coefficient of correlation (r) between the first and second scores for individuals in the uncertain task settings was 0.691, and for individuals in the certain task settings it was 0.727. The statistical significance of difference in means for the two kinds of settings: one-tailed probability, $F = 7.5120$; $p = < 0.001$.

[b] The statistical significance of difference in overall means for the two kinds of settings: one-tailed probability, $t = 5.36$; $p = < 0.001$.

[c] The higher the score, the more autonomy, freedom, and independence in authority relations is preferred. The statistical significance of the difference in overall means for the two kinds of settings: one-tailed probability, $t = 10.96$; $p = < 0.001$.

[d] The higher the score, the more the individual prefers to work alone. The lower the score, the more the individual prefers to work and spend time in groups. The statistical significance of the difference in overall means for the two kinds of settings: one-tailed probability: $t = 6.37$; $p = < 0.001$.

TABLE 3-5 Similarities in Personality Dimensions of Members in High- and Low-performing Sites in an Uncertain Research Environment [a]

Type of laboratory	Performance	
Communications laboratories	High performer	Low performer
Integrative complexity	5.20	5.19
Tolerance for ambiguity	2.93	2.98
Attitude toward authority	2.68	2.78
Attitude toward individualism	3.01	2.95
Medical laboratories	High performer	Low performer
Integrative complexity	5.37	5.27
Tolerance for ambiguity	2.79	2.83
Attitude toward authority	2.82	2.91
Attitude toward individualism	2.96	2.90
Drug laboratories	High performer	Low performer
Integrative complexity	5.27	5.10
Tolerance for ambiguity	2.93	2.91
Attitude toward authority	2.75	2.82
Attitude toward individualism	2.97	2.92

	All high-performing sites	All low-performing sites	Overall mean
Integrative complexity	5.23	5.15	5.20
Tolerance for ambiguity	2.90	2.91	2.91
Attitude toward authority	2.76	2.88	2.83
Attitude toward individualism	2.99	2.95	2.96

[a] The differences in means between high- and low-performing sites were *not* significant at the 0.1 level for any of the four dimensions. The N for integrative complexity: all high-performing sites, $N = 75$; all low-performing sites, $N = 73$. The N for all other dimensions: all high-performing sites, $N = 50$; all low-performing sites, $N = 42$.

preferred to work alone rather than in groups. In the production sites in the stable, shorter-term environment, people had a lower tolerance for ambiguity, were comfortable working under more controlling authority figures, and preferred to work in groups rather than alone. All of these differences were statistically significant, as is shown in Fig. 3-6.

It is important to reemphasize that these differences existed among all members of the production plants and research laboratories regardless of the performance level of the sites. That is, there were *no* statistically significant differences between members of high- and low-performing units of either type along these dimensions. Even though members' personality dimensions suited the requirements for environmental mastery in the low-performing sites in both types of environment, members had significantly lower feelings of competence and the sites themselves were less effective performers. This complicates our explanation of differences in members' sense of competence and in the performance of the pairs of sites. For an explanation, we must look beyond a congruence of external environment requirements and members' personality dimensions. As a way of wrestling with this dilemma, let us summarize our data concerning members' characteristics and our expectations about them, and review our three alternative explanations of why members in high-performing sites in both environments felt more competent than members in low-performing sites.

Members' Characteristics and the External Environment: A Summary

In Table 3-6, our expectations about organization members' characteristics are compared with our findings. As we have seen, unit members' four personality dimensions discriminate well between people dealing with manufacturing external environments and those dealing with research external environments. The discrimination on the basis of the four dimensions, however, does not help us fully to understand the differences in our other major criterion variable, the level of performance within each type of organization unit. Table 3-6 indicates that members' sense of competence discriminates well between members of high-performing units and those of low-performing units. So far our data about feelings of competence does not help us fully to understand how variations in these feelings might be related to the differences in the nature of the external environment. We need an expanded

TABLE 3-6 Revisiting the Fit of Environmental Requirements and Members' Personality Dimensions with Sense of Competence

	Certain environment	*a discriminates, but not b*	Uncertain environment	
	Expectations	Data	Expectations	Data
High performing	Low integrative complexity	Low [a]	High integrative complexity	High [a]
	Low tolerance for ambiguity	Low [a]	High tolerance for ambiguity	High [a]
	Low attitude toward authority	Low [a]	High attitude toward authority	High [a]
	Low attitude toward individualism	Low [a]	High attitude toward individualism	High [a]
b discriminates, but not a	High sense of competence	High [b]	High sense of competence	High [b]
Low performing	High integrative complexity	Low [a]	Low integrative complexity	High [a]
	High tolerance for ambiguity	Low [a]	Low tolerance for ambiguity	High [a]
	High attitude toward authority	Low [a]	Low attitude toward authority	High [a]
	High attitude toward individualism	Low [a]	Low attitude toward individualism	High [a]
	Low sense of competence	Low [b]	Low sense of competence	Low [b]

[a] indicates *actual* differences in members' integrative complexity, tolerance for ambiguity, attitude toward authority, and attitude toward individualism.

There were *no* statistically significant differences between members in high- and low-performing sites in both environments on any of the four dimensions. *Across* the two types of environment, all differences in dimensions were significant at < 0.001.

[b] indicates *actual* differences in members' sense of competence. Differences in members' feelings of competence in each high-performing vs. low-performing pair of sites were significant at < 0.01 in all pairs but one (significant at < 0.02).

framework to further our understanding of how differences in our two criterion variables, the nature of the environment and unit performance, are simultaneously related to differences in members' feelings of competence.

Earlier we gave three possible explanations why a high sense of competence might be related to high performance. We suggested that high-performing units might attract people with already strong feelings of competence; that high performance provided information and feedback that enhanced members' confidence in their competence; and that a fit between external environmental requirements and members' personality dimensions influenced the relationship. All three seem to be reasonable and plausible explanations. From the data summarized in Table 3-6, we have findings that are not inconsistent with the first two explanations, but do not support the notion that a contingency fit beween members' personalities and the external environment is related to a high sense of competence and high performance. Organization unit members in *all* of the sites in the manufacturing environment tended to have predispositions suited to their environment. Organization members in *all* of the sites in the research environment also tended toward predispositions suited to their environment. But a match between members' personality dimensions and the external environment was related to high feelings of competence only in the high-performing sites. Even though there was a match between members' predispositions and their external environment in the other sites, it was associated with low feelings of competence and low performance. We need to investigate why the match found in the low-performing sites was not related, as it was in the high performers, to high feelings of competence and effective performance.

If the theoretical perspective outlined in Chapter 1 is valid, we would expect that it would be helpful to examine whether the internal environment of the organization fits better with the external environment and members' predispositions in the high-performing sites than it does in the less effective ones. It is important to take this step even though we accept the notion that people with a strong sense of competence may be attracted to high-performing units and that high performance itself feeds members' feelings of competence. However, neither of these explanations is as useful as the fit argument from the practical perspective of improving organizational effectiveness and enhancing the individual's feelings about himself at work. If a manager, struggling with a low-performing unit, sets out to find and attract persons with a strong sense of competence to his unit, they might not find it an attractive place in which to work. Further, these strong feelings of competence mean that the individual expects to be competent and he, therefore, even if attracted to the low-performing unit, might find working in it very frustrating, even for a turn-around period. On the other hand, if the manager sets out to deal with his problem by trying to improve unit performance, he must learn how to manage and organize his personnel more effectively. This is what the "fit" possibility is all about and what makes it so important in our understanding of the problem.

4

The internal environment
of manufacturing plants

In this chapter we will consider data about the internal environment. The internal environment can be thought of as man's implicit and explicit social invention to help members relate to the work of the organization in dealing with the external environment. This and the next chapter will show just how this occurs and why the contingency theory of organizations must consider a three-way fit of people and the external and the internal environments in order to understand the feelings of competence and performance in a particular unit.

Organization Members and Internal Environments of Production Units

Table 4-1 summarizes our findings from Chapter 3 about members' characteristics in manufacturing environments and lists the elements of the organization's internal environment studied in the production plants, as well as the laboratories. In addition to investigating members' time and goal orientations, for which Lawrence and Lorsch have developed a methodology, we have investigated members' influence and control over their own

TABLE 4-1 Members' Characteristics in the Production Plants and the Internal Environment Variables Studied

	Certain external environment	
	Members' data	
	Low integrative complexity	
	Low tolerance for ambiguity	
	Low attitude toward authority (not uncomfortable in strong, controlling authority relations)	
	Low attitude toward individualism (prefers to be and work in groups)	
	High sense of competence	
	Internal environmental variables studied	
High-performing plants	Time orientation	
	Goal orientation	
	Influence and control: Formality of structure Perceptions of the influence and control pattern: amount and pattern of structure and influence Perceptions of "say" and supervisory style	
	Coordination of work activities: Formality of structure Perceptions of coordination achieved Mode of conflict resolution	

and others' work activities and the degree of coordination of work activities.[1] Members' influence and control was measured by the degree of formality of structure in the internal environment, as well as by members' own perceptions of the influence pattern and supervisory style characteristics of the internal environment. Data about intraunit coordination was gathered by looking again at the formality of structure and also at members' perceptions of the coordination achieved and the mode of conflict resolution used to achieve such coordination. The methodology used to collect all these data is explained in more detail in the "Methodological Appendix."

We shall relate these internal environment variables, not only to the

[1] Paul R. Lawrence and Jay W. Lorsch, "Methodological Appendix," in *Organization and Environment* (Boston: Harvard Business School, Division of Research, 1967).

	Certain external environment
	Members' data
	Low integrative complexity
	Low tolerance for ambiguity
	Low attitude toward authority (not uncomfortable in strong, controlling authority relations)
	Low attitude toward individualism (prefers to be and work in groups)
	Low sense of competence
	Internal environmental variables studied
Low- *performing* *plants*	Time orientation
	Goal orientation

	Influence and control:
	    Formality of structure
	    Perceptions of the influence and control pattern: amount and
	       pattern of structure and influence
	    Perceptions of "say" and supervisory style

	Coordination of work activities:
	    Formality of structure
	    Perceptions of coordination achieved
	    Mode of conflict resolution

---

external environment and total organizational performance as Lawrence and Lorsch did, but also to organization members' characteristics, effective performance of each unit, and sense of competence of unit members. We will consider each internal environmental variable in turn with this complex system of relationships in mind.

Members' Time and Goal Orientations

The management practices in both high- and low-performing plants emphasized daily reviews of performance and daily reports of plant activities. It was not unusual for all plants to supplement these daily reviews and reports with hourly ones wherever a problem existed. Top managers in both high- and low-performing plants indicated their interest in daily and hourly results by publishing them on blackboards around the plant for all to see, sending out mimeographed summaries before the close of each day for supervisors to peruse, and expecting subordinates to have the latest production and cost figures available at even chance meetings with superiors on the plant floor. With the extremely short-term nature of the manufacturing environment and the rapid feedback about performance, it was difficult to see how a plant could emphasize anything but a short-term time frame. Trouble had to be spotted almost as soon as it occurred so that immediate corrective action could be taken to keep the lines running smoothly.

As is shown in Table 4-2, these formal practices—the requirements from the external environment for a short-term time orientation and members' low tolerance for ambiguity—were associated with almost an identically strong short-term time orientation for members of both high- and low-performing plants. All personnel indicated a strong concern for short-term performance criteria and feedback, which was consistent with the requirements of the external environment and their own personality preferences. Therefore, it is doubtful that time-orientation differences in the plants led to differences in members' activities resulting in variations in unit effectiveness or members' feelings of competence.

TABLE 4-2 Members' Time Orientations in the Manufacturing Plants

	Time orientation			
Type of plant	1 month or less	1-3 months	3-12 months	1-5 years
Effective container plant	62%	17%	13%	8%
Effective appliance plant	57	21	14	8
Less effective container plant	57	22	13	8
Less effective appliance plant	60	22	17	1

The statistical significance of differences in pairs of plants and between all high-performing plants and all lower-performing plants was not significant at the 0.05 level.

The percentages indicate the percentage of managers and supervisors in the plants perceiving themselves to be working on problems reaching fruition in the time period specified. The total number of respondents providing the data about members' own perceptions and experiences of their internal environment was the same as the number of those responding to the tests measuring sense of competence as reported in Chapter 3.

Regarding goal orientations in the plants, a different picture emerged. Members of the effective plants clearly indicated a particularly high concern for technical, cost/economics, efficiency and production goals, having a lesser concern for scientific ones. As is shown in Table 4-3, those in the less effective plants, although on the whole more concerned with these same techno-economic goals than with sales or scientific goals, nonetheless showed significantly lower concern for techno-economic goals than did the members of the effective plants. Interestingly enough, the secondary goal orientation in all the plants except the low-performing container plants was a concern for marketing or sales goals, which seems consistent with the customer orientation that even the most technically proficient plant must have. A manager in the less effective container plant explained why his colleagues showed relatively more concern for scientific goals than for sales goals:

> It's difficult to increase your volume of business with your customers. They tend to parcel out so much to us and so much to our competitors because they have to keep a number of suppliers available. So we believe that one of the best ways that we can improve our performance is to get new products, new materials, new ways of sealing and opening the container, etc. A few good, new ideas could take us right to the top of the company. But it's difficult to develop new technical products in this mature industry. We sell a fairly standard item, so we really need some good hard thought on how to improve it.

TABLE 4-3 Members' Goal Orientations in the Manufacturing Plants [a]

Type of plant	Techno-economic	Marketing	Scientific
Effective container plant	1.35	2.05	2.59
Effective appliance plant	1.33	2.15	2.51
Less effective container plant	1.50	2.26	2.24
Less effective appliance plant	1.83	2.00	2.17

[a] Lower score indicates *more* concern for goal.

The statistical significance of difference in means between effective and less effective plants (all one-tailed probabilities):

	Techno-economic	Marketing	Scientific
Appliance plants	$t = 6.68$; $p = < 0.001$	$t = 2.86$; $p = < 0.01$	$t = 3.79$; $p = < 0.001$
Container plants	$t = 2.10$; $p = < 0.05$	$t = 2.59$; $p = < 0.02$	$t = 5.84$; $p = < 0.001$

As seen in this plant, the developing of new materials and processes was a means of boosting the plant's track record and this probably resulted in the otherwise inexplicable concern for scientific goals, but, as the manager suggests, it may be a dubious strategy in such an environment.

In summary, all high- and low-performing plants had an internal environment oriented to short-term goals. This was appropriate to both the external environmental requirements and to members' relatively low tolerance for ambiguity. There were, nonetheless, significant differences among members in the high and low performers in goal orientations, which meant that only individuals in high-performing plants had developed the solid short-term concerns for production goals that fit the environment as well as their personal predispositions. These orientations probably helped to account in part, not only for higher unit performance, but also for members' greater feelings of competence since these individuals preferred to gain their sense of competence from dealing with less ambiguous situations.

Members' Influence and Control over Work Activities

How much influence and control members had over their own and others' work activities was measured by (1) the degree of formality of structure within the internal environment (was there high reliance on formal rules, procedures, and controls, and tight spans of control, or was this absent?); (2) by members' own perceptions of the degree of structure within the internal environment; (3) by the amount of total influence being exercised in the unit and at what hierarchical levels; (4) by the amount of "say" members had in choosing and handling work activities on their own; and (5) by the type of supervision in the internal environment.

The formal structure in the manufacturing plants

Both of the large companies from which the two pairs of production plants were selected had defined tight plant organization structures and rigid plant operating rules, procedures, and controls on a company-wide basis. Thus, all four manufacturing and assembly plants had relatively rigid and clearly defined patterns of formal relationships and comprehensive rules and procedures, which fit the certainty of the external environment and the members' low integrative complexity and tolerance for ambiguity. Consistent with the information in the external environment, which was clear, unambiguous, and slow to change, the two large companies that operated the four plants had defined a highly formalized structure which people who processed information at a low level of complexity and who were comfortable with unambiguous settings might prefer.

In spite of such similarities in all four sites, our own observations and interviews with plant personnel revealed differences between high- and low-performing sites in the day-to-day *use* of the company-defined formal structure and procedures. Managers in the less successful plants, more often than those in the effective plants, indicated that they had to work "around" and not "through" the formal structure to get the job done. They also indicated a definite lack of consensus as to the content of many of the managerial positions. One manager in the less effective container plant said:

> I guess I'd have to say we don't follow the chain of command or the organization chart that much here. You can often get better and faster information by going "around" the chain of command than you can by going through it. The information I need for a decision often doesn't exist at the place the organization chart says it's supposed to, so I go to where it is. After a while, you learn where the information you need exists and you look for it there and not by looking at the formal organization chart. Also, the regular formal channels around here are often stopped up and this isn't the kind of business where you can sit and wait for them to clear up, so we have to use other channels to get things done.

A supervisor in the low-performing appliance plant was more succinct, but no less emphatic:

> The organization chart and chain of command set up too much interference to work through here. Consequently, we do a lot of bypassing of levels to get the job done. Top level managers will go right to the first-line foreman or to the line worker himself. You could heave the organization charts out the window or tip them upside down—that's how much use we make of them.

In contrast, managers in the successful sites jealously guarded their normal chain of command and agreed that working through it and not around it was the way to operate. They also saw managerial positions as precisely defined and these definitions were stringently followed. Quoting one executive in the high-performing container plant:

> This plant stresses knowing who's responsible for what. Each man is responsible for all aspects of his particular job, and only for those aspects. Each man in the plant knows the extent and limits of his job, and everyone else in the plant knows the same thing, that is, who to see about a particular problem and *only* that particular problem. We work through assigned responsibility

here. Everybody knows what's expected of everyone else. If a man is expected to handle a job or have some information and he doesn't, well, he'll be harassed and kidded until he lives up to expectations.

Summarizing the differences in the plants' formal structure: the successful performers had formal job descriptions, duties, rules, procedures, and control systems that were comprehensive, precisely defined, and uniformly enforced throughout the organization. On the continuum from high to low formality of structure, the four plants fell into the grid indicated in Fig. 4-1.

Fig. 4-1. The formal structure in the manufacturing plants.[a]

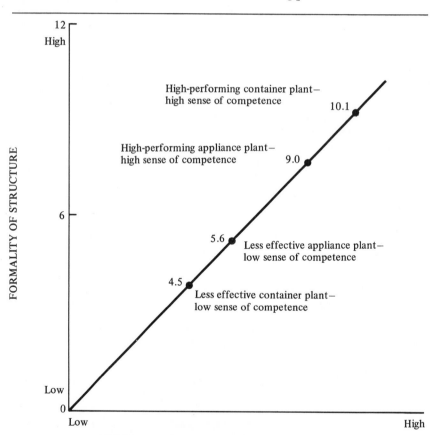

FORMALITY OF STRUCTURE

12 High

High-performing container plant— high sense of competence 10.1

High-performing appliance plant— high sense of competence 9.0

6

5.6 Less effective appliance plant— low sense of competence

4.5 Less effective container plant— low sense of competence

Low

0

Low   High

PERFORMANCE AND MEMBERS' SENSE OF COMPETENCE

[a] Average scores for Sections 1, 2, and 3 of the "Researcher's Data Sheet for Unit Formal Practices" were simply added together to position a site on the grid.

The data for making the judgment about formality of structure were collected through Sections 1, 2, and 3 of the "Researcher's Data Sheet for Unit Formal Practices," described in the "Methodological Appendix." Significantly, it was only in the sites where formal structure matched both the external environment and members' predispositions that system performance was high and people experienced the reward of a strong sense of competence.

Through this high degree of formal structure, the work activities of members was clearly defined and unambiguous. In the less successful plants, formal practices in use were much looser and not uniformly enforced. This seemed to be related to more deviations, ambiguities, and inconsistencies in work activities in an external environment that demanded just the opposite. Thus, the more formal structure which we found in the effective plants seemed to fit the certain external environment because one of the critical elements for success in the production environment involved ensuring that each member performed the well-defined work activities that were required of him around the precisely defined technology. More formal control was also essentially a way of programming activities and was preferred by members of these units who had a low tolerance for ambiguity and lower integrative complexity. The use of formal control devices in the successful plants, therefore, not only matched the external environment, but also members' personality dimensions, while the use of formal controls in the less effective plants matched neither as well.

Members' perceptions of the influence and control patterns

The differences in formal structure in the plants seemed to be connected to differences in the *perceptions* of plant members about the pattern of influence and control in the internal environment. Because people often act as they perceive, differences in these perceptions could greatly affect organization performance and members' feelings of competence.[2] The data in Fig. 4-2 reflects that members in the successful plants perceived more structure in the internal environment and perceived their work activities to be more standardized and well defined than did their counterparts in the less effective plants. A supervisor in the effective container plant stressed, "We have rules and standards dealing with everything from how much powder to

[3] Donald Snygg and Arthur W. Combs, *Individual Behavior* (New York: Harper & Row, 1949).

Fig. 4-2. Members' perceptions of the degree of structure in the plants.

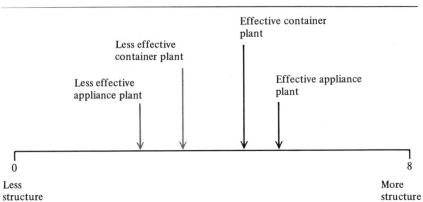

Scores for the members' perceptions of degree of structure were obtained by combining scores for the perceptions of (1) behavioral conformity and (2) organizational clarity in the plants. Scores for each plant are indicated below. Higher score signifies perceptions of more structure.

Type of plant	Conformity	Clarity	Total structure
Effective appliance plant ($N = 39$)	2.95	3.25	6.20
Effective container plant ($N = 30$)	2.70	3.46	6.16
Less effective container plant ($N = 28$)	2.37	2.64	5.01
Less effective appliance plant ($N = 41$)	2.23	2.29	4.52

The statistical significance of difference in means between high and low performers (all one-tailed probabilities):

	Conformity	Clarity	Total structure
Appliance plants	$t = 7.96; p = < 0.001$	$t = 10.40; p = < 0.001$	$t = 13.21; p = < 0.001$
Container plants	$t = 3.65; p = < 0.001$	$t = 5.06; p = < 0.001$	$t = 6.74; p = < 0.001$

use in cleaning out toilet bowls to how to cart a dead body out of the plant. Everyone is subject to them . . . there are no exceptions."

The greater reliance on working through the organization structure and the greater uniformity and consistency of rules and procedures in the effective plants apparently helped to account for these perceptions of higher structure. In turn, these perceptions reinforced the relatively uniform and standardized work activities that were suited to the requirements of the external environment and to people with relatively low integrative complexity and tolerance for ambiguity. One executive in the successful appliance plant illustrated the importance of this, "People here can't object to changing shifts on time, taking breaks on time, etc., so that the assembly lines won't run with nothing on them. We lose money when lines run unattended or with empty slots, so we don't let that happen here."

Quite different tendencies characterized the less effective plants. Members perceived lower formality of structure, conformity, and organization clarity, which meant that work activities were more ambiguous and, as a consequence, less appropriate to the certain external environment and to members' predispositions.

The high- and low-performing plants also differed in the total amount of influence exercised, and in the distribution of this influence. Members in the effective plants perceived less total influence in their organizations than did members of the less effective plants. As Figs. 4-3 and 4-4 show, this was because, in the high-performing plants, influence was more heavily concentrated at upper levels, while in the less effective plants it was more evenly distributed through all levels.

In the successful plants, less total influence and influence concentrated in the upper levels of the hierarchy indicated that more decision-making was taking place at the top of the organization. This seems to fit the manufacturing environment where information to make many decisions can be assembled at the top and it would also fit the plant personnel who were not uncomfortable with relatively strong authority relations in which superiors made many decisons. Because the major competitive issues for these plants were meeting production and delivery schedules and enforcing quality and cost standards, and because the information to make such decisions was quite certain, it was more effective to make decisions at the top. At planning meetings in the two high performers, the respective chief executives typically made decisions on the prime competitive concerns, using external environmental information that no one else in the plants could easily obtain. For example, the top man in the successful appliance plant provided intimate knowledge of the corporate budgeting process and production standards-setting process as background for his major cost and production scheduling decisions. Similarly, the plant manager in the successful container plant explained at one point in a planning session that a new manager had just been installed in their principal customer's plant and that he had decided on the basis of this information "to flood him with containers so that he'll

Fig. 4-3. Amount of influence in the plants.

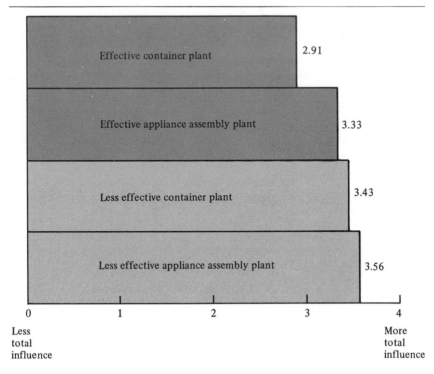

Effective container plant   2.91

Effective appliance assembly plant   3.33

Less effective container plant   3.43

Less effective appliance assembly plant   3.56

0   1   2   3   4

Less total influence   More total influence

Scores reported are the means for each plant. Lower scores indicate perceptions of lower total influence exercised in the plant. The statistical significance of difference in means (all one-tailed probabilities):

Appliance plants	$t = 2.48;\ p = < 0.02$
Container plants	$t = 2.50;\ p = < 0.02$

get the message quickly that we're the best supplier he has available to him." While this pattern existed in the effective plants, the low performers practiced decision-making at more diffuse levels in the organization. But, members at lower organizational levels in these plants could not easily obtain (and in some cases simply did not have) knowledge of the external environment necessary to make effective decisions. Likewise, it is doubtful that the members of the low-performing plants would have been uncomfortable about having superiors take the responsibility for complex decisions, because

Fig. 4-4. Distribution of influence in the plants.

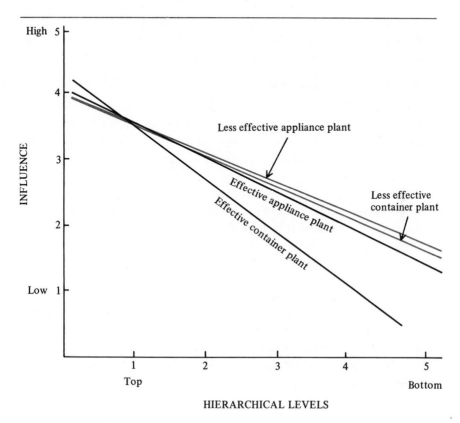

Lines fitted by least-squares method, with the model $Y=BX+A$. Regression equations for each line were:

Highly effective container plant	$Y = -0.66X + 4.3$
Highly effective appliance plant	$Y = -0.39X + 4.22$
Less effective container plant	$Y = -0.37X + 3.83$
Less effective appliance plant	$Y = -0.34X + 3.99$

The statistical significance of difference in slopes (one-tailed probabilities):

The appliance plants	$t = 3.87; p = < 0.01$
The container plants	$t = 33.27; p = < 0.001$

The steeper the line, the more hierarchical the distribution of influence. The flatter the line, the more egalitarian the distribution of influence.

of their preference for dealing with stronger authority figures. So, when the influence and control pattern matched the external environment and members' personality dimensions, we found high performance and strong feelings of competence. When there was less of a match, there was lower performance and a lower sense of competence.

"Say" and supervisory style

Given these data about differing patterns of influence and control, it is not surprising that members in the high-performing plants perceived themselves to have less say in choosing and handling work activities, describing the type of supervision as being more directive than participatory or laissez-faire than did the members of the less effective plants. The data in Tables 4-4 and 4-5 indicate these perceptions.[3] In the high-performing plants, many decisions were made by superiors who had less discussion with subordinates. However, it is important to note that lower-level managers in these effective plants were not totally excluded from participating in decisions. In fact, there appeared to be a balance between directive and participative supervision, with lower-level managers participating in those decisions to which they could contribute. In the low performing plants, however, individuals felt they had more say in selecting and handling tasks (and described the type of supervision as highly participative), than did their counterparts in the effective sites. Here, more mutual decisions were made after superior-subordinate discussions. The say and supervisory patterns in the high performers seemed to contribute to effectiveness and strong feelings of competence since they matched the requirements of the external environment and members' personality dimensions. With regard to the external environment, the patterns appropriately reflected the certainty of the two major kinds of knowledge needed to deal with the environment. One kind of knowledge centered on the technology of the production process itself and was highly defined once the automated lines were set up. The lines incorporated the technical knowledge of how to do the tasks, thereby relieving members of the necessity of making one set of critical decisions. The other kind of knowledge centered on the overall scheduling and budgeting of the plant to produce quality items on schedule and within

---

[3] A *participative* type of supervision would mean that subordinates saw themselves as consulting with superiors before decisions were jointly made. *Directive* supervision implied much less superior-subordinate consultation, with the supervisor making most of the decisions. *Laissez-faire* supervision meant that there was no superior-subordinate consultation, with the subordinate making most of the decisions.

TABLE 4-4 Freedom and Autonomy to Choose and Handle Work Activities in the Plants

Type of plant	Say in initially choosing own work		
	High	Medium	Low
Effective container plant	17%	28%	55%
Effective appliance plant	23	37	40
Less effective container plant	47	39	14
Less effective appliance plant	67	28	5

The percentages refer to the percentage of respondents indicating each category. The total number of respondents in each plant was the same as the number of respondents to the tests measuring sense of competence, as reported in Chapter 3. Converting the percentages to numbers of respondents in each category results in the following statistical significance of differences in the plants (chi-square distribution):

Appliance plants	$\chi^2 = 20.01$; $p = < 0.001$
Container plants	$\chi^2 = 13.52$; $p = < 0.001$

	Say in handling work on own once chosen		
	High	Medium	Low
Effective container plant	24%	55%	21%
Effective appliance plant	47	45	8
Less effective container plant	75	18	7
Less effective appliance plant	85	15	0

The percentages again refer to the percentage of respondents indicating each category. The statistical significance of differences in the pairs of plants, using the conversion process cited above (chi-square distribution):

Appliance plants	$\chi^2 = 14.41$; $p = < 0.001$
Container plants	$\chi^2 = 14.25$; $p = < 0.001$

cost constraints. This knowledge was generally quite certain also and, as we have seen, could be easily handled by the top level of plant executives. So far as personality predispositions are concerned, members themselves, because of their attitudes toward authority and their low tolerance for ambiguity, did not seem to mind a setting in which well-defined decisions were made by superiors. In the less effective plants where members had identical personality predispositions there was an attempt to obtain more

TABLE 4-5 Type of Supervision in the Plants

Type of plant	Directive	Participative	Laissez-faire
Effective container plant	45%	48%	7%
Effective appliance plant	47	41	12
Less effective container plant	4	87	9
Less effective appliance plant	2	78	20

The percentages refer to the percentage of respondents indicating each category. The statistical significance of differences in number of respondents in each pair of plants (chi-square distribution):

Appliance plants	$\chi^2 = 21.20$; $p = \ < 0.001$
Container plants	$\chi^2 = 14.05$; $p = \ < 0.001$

joint discussion and decision-making. But, a supervisor in the low-performing appliance plant expressed some typical frustrations about such behavior: "We have meetings, meetings, meetings. Whenever there's a problem, however small, we have a meeting to solve it. Everybody meets on everything to try to get agreement—but nobody makes decisions!"

It appears that too much discussion and mutual decision-making is time-consuming and does not lead to better decision-making in such an environment. Nor does it fit with the predispositions of these organization members. This is not to say that all participation by lower-level managers in decision-making was inappropriate. Certainly in decisions concerning major changes in procedures and practices, the involvement of lower-level managers in decision-making would be helpful in building commitment to major decisions. As Vroom has pointed out, such participation leads members to a feeling of "owning" decisions.[4] However, in the case of the low-performing plants our data suggest that the participative leadership and decision-making was so excessive that the internal environment met neither the requirements of the external environment nor the predispositions of unit members. In the effective plants, such participation was balanced with strong direction from top management which, as we have seen, better fit all aspects of the situations.

[4] Victor H. Vroom, *Some Personality Determinants of the Effects of Participation* (Englewood Cliffs, N.J.: Prentice-Hall, 1960).

Coordination of work activities

In Chapter 2, we emphasized the need for a high degree of coordination of members' activity in this external environment. Briefly, both pairs of plants relied on continuous-fed, high-speed production lines that were scheduled by a centralized group. It was vital for the successful performance of the plants that each member know exactly what was expected of him and that he integrate his work behavior closely with other members of the managerial and professional team. In practice, high-performing plants alone had developed a high degree of formal structure that facilitated coordination and cooperation. The less effective plants, as described earlier in this chapter, had less uniformity and standardization in work rules and procedures. This point and its impact on coordination is emphasized by a supervisor in the less effective container plant:

> Sure, we've got work and manufacturing rules and procedures and instructions that everybody follows. We couldn't make a container if we didn't. But you'll find each department and each shift its own bailiwick when it comes to rules on breaks, discipline, overtime, and the like. Each manager in each department negotiates his own set of rules and practices for his people, and when he leaves, his successor inherits all of these old negotiated rules and then negotiates his own. We've got five or six separate companies here, each with its own outlook and own set of rules. We're not a team, we're not coordinated and controlled uniformly across the board, and we won't be until we can get uniformity among departments and shifts on these rules and formal practices.

As this manager implied, the lack of uniformity and standardization in the less effective plants tended to lead to less coordination in an external environment where coordination was important. Because departments within the plants were developing their own rules and procedures concerning important elements of the work environment, already-existing job differences among departments were even more difficult to coordinate and bring together toward overall plant goals. The high degree of formality of structure which facilitated coordinated team effort in the effective plants was also congruent with members' attitudes toward working with others. Members of both high- and low-performing plants indicated a preference to be and work in highly coordinated groups. The high-performing sites where members had strong feelings of competence provided the formal structure which facilitated a high level of member coordination.

Perceptions of the coordination of work effort achieved among members differed between high- and low-performing plants in a way which was consistent with the differences in the formality of structure. As the discussion above indicates and Table 4-6 shows, the higher degree of formality of structure in the effective plants was associated with achieving a significantly higher degree of coordination of work activities among colleagues. A manager in the effective appliance plant recognized how well this high level of coordination fit the external environment:

> Without a high level of coordination among departments and individuals in the plant, we couldn't put out a quality appliance at low cost. When you go through this plant, you might be overwhelmed by the control systems, reports, evaluation systems, and rules. There are a lot of them and they're used here. They're necessary to make certain that everybody is getting together and coordinating their individual jobs toward the overall performance goals of the plant. This control and coordination doesn't just happen. Top managers here insist on real coordination of people and departments. They have made it a plant rule to stress cooperation and teamwork. [The formal] rules and control systems help, but it's more the top managers' insistence and concern that makes the coordination a reality in the plant. We have also developed what we call "brother relationships" in the plant. When a problem arises in one department that requires the help of another department, we expect the supervisor responsible for handling the problem to coordinate with his "brother" [or counterpart] in the other department. Supervisors know they're evaluated on how well they coordinate and cooperate with other supervisors and other departments.

Such coordinative activities as we have suggested were also consistent with plant personnel's preference for working closely with others.

Lower coordination of effort in the less effective plants resulted in more fragmented and less uniform work activities that were difficult to unify around the production processes. Members described the frustrations they encountered with lower coordination:

TABLE 4-6 Coordination of Work Effort Achieved in the Plants

Type of plant	High	Medium	Low
Effective container plant	87%	10%	3%
Effective appliance plant	89	8	3
Less effective container plant	60	36	4
Less effective appliance plant	58	32	10

The percentages refer to the percentage of respondents indicating each category. The statistical significance of difference in number of respondents in each pair of plants (chi-square distribution):

Appliance plants	$\chi^2 = 10.06; p = < 0.01$
Container plants	$\chi^2 = 6.90; p = < 0.02$

There's no doubt that there's a definite lack of cooperation among areas and among individuals in our appliance plant. We don't communicate or coordinate enough so that we are not able to anticipate changes or problems that arise in departments that work on the appliance frame before it gets to us. This leads to a lack of results and a lackadaisical attitude on the part of the workers and managers.

The name of the game in our plant is "passing the buck," that is, if a preceding department makes a mistake or doesn't complete a job, it sends the problem frame on anyway and hopes that it's caught and corrected in later departments. There's too much of that going on here. We ought to be working together, but we cut each other's throats by sending problems on to the next departments. It makes the latter departments look bad on performance just to save the skin of some supervisor in earlier departments in the process flow. You won't get coordination among departments until this stops.

Mode of Conflict Resolution

Given the external environmental requirement for a high degree of co-ordination of work effort and members' predispositions to be and work in groups, and yet given the inevitable conflicts that arise among different groups in the plant, the characteristic mode of resolving conflict becomes important. Different approaches to conflict resolution can be categorized as confrontation, forcing, and smoothing.[5] Behaving in the confrontation mode means that individuals attempt to find the basis for the conflict and ways of resolving underlying issues. In the forcing mode, individuals try to win their own positions, at the expense of the other parties to the conflict. They fight for their own positions through the use of power. And, in the smoothing mode, individuals either avoid generating conflict or try to smooth feelings and keep people together when it does occur. In the effective appliance plant, managers and supervisors described their typical behavior in resolving conflicts as confrontation, that is, they pushed to find and resolve the underlying reasons for the conflict. As Table 4-7 shows, individuals in the low-performing appliance plant most often forced the solution of conflicts, that is, they tried to win their own positions through power gambits. Although questionnaire data concerning the mode of conflict resolution in the container plants were lacking because we did not appreciate the importance of this variable until we had analyzed the clinical data from those plants, we can use some of that interview data to suggest

[5] Robert Blake and Jane Mouton, in *The Managerial Grid* (Houston: Gulf, 1964) recognize the modes of conflict resolution. In addition to the three measured in this study, they identify *compromise* and *withdrawal* as additional modes.

TABLE 4-7 Modes of Conflict Resolution in the Plants [a]

Type of plant	Confrontation	Forcing	Smoothing
Effective container plant	No data	No data	No data
Effective appliance plant	2.36 [b]	3.05	3.42
Less effective container plant	No data	No data	No data
Less effective appliance plant	2.76	2.45 [b]	3.17

[a] Lower score indicates *more* use of mode. Data for these variables were not collected in the two container plants.

[b] Dominant mode of conflict resolution in the plant, that is, the behavior most typically used to solve problems and achieve coordination.

The statistical significance of difference in means (all one-tailed probabilities):

	Confrontation	Forcing	Smoothing
Appliance plants	$t = 2.30$; $p = 0.02$	$t = 2.76$; $p = < 0.01$	Not significant at 0.05 level

that confrontation also characterized the highly effective container plant. An executive there said:

> It's important that when we find solutions to problems of coordination and cooperation that we don't just find what I call "surface solutions," that is, solutions that get us through another hectic day but that don't get the real issues at stake. So, I push my subordinates and my staff to get at the heart of the problem and resolve the issue once and for all. We're not in the kind of business where you can afford to have past "surface solutions" come back to haunt you in your current operations.

Thus, both high-performing plants appeared to be resolving conflict through confrontation. These findings take on a special import when combined with the earlier findings concerning the use of a more directive supervisory style in the successful plants. It did not necessarily follow because more directive supervision was utilized in these plants that subordinates felt they were coerced or forced into conflict resolution. Apparently, a more directive style was not seen as leading to coercion or the inappropriate use of power. We can speculate that at least two factors led to this result. First, as we pointed out above, lower-level managers in these effective plants did participate in decisions where they had knowledge to contribute. Second, and related to this, the directive leadership made sense to lower-level managers with their preference for stronger authority relationship in a highly certain external environment.

Summary of Members' Characteristics and the External and Internal Environments in the Plants

Summarizing our findings about members' personality characteristics in the manufacturing environment and our findings about the internal environments of the high- and low-performing sites, we can see that by including the internal environment in our considerations we are able to explain why high feelings of competence are related to high performance. See Table 4-8 for a summary of our findings. In the manufacturing sites, a three-way fit among the people, the external environment, and the internal organization environment was associated with high feelings of competence and high unit performance.

The lower integrative complexity which characterized the members of the plants fits the higher certainty of information in their external environment. Feedback about performance was swift, specific, and unambiguous. Organizations dealing with such an external environment needed an internal environment which defined many precise formal rules for information-processing and developed a relatively formal hierarchy. Individuals with lower-integrative complexity would prefer to use these more fixed, externally defined rules in the internal environment for sensing and responding to external environmental information, rather than relying on their own interpretations of task situations. The relatively low tolerance for ambiguity of the production members also fits the precision and rapidity of performance feedback from the external environment and the high formality of organization in the internal environment. In addition, because critical information about the external environment was either programmed into the automated technology itself or left to the top levels in the hierarchy, individuals needed only a low ability to tolerate change and ambiguity. Similarly, the tight controls and rigid scheduling that should be a part of the internal environment of a unit dealing with a predictable external environment also made sense to people with a relatively low tolerance for ambiguity.

In terms of attitudes toward authority, the members of the plants felt comfortable with somewhat less autonomy and with somewhat more dependent authority relations. This also suited an external environment which required that the internal environment provide comprehensive definitions of, and restrictions on, work behavior, decision-making at higher levels in the hierarchy, and more directive supervision. With their preferences for relatively strong authority relations, individuals working in the certain environment did not feel overly controlled or coerced by rules and instructions in

TABLE 4-8 Members' Characteristics and Internal Organization Environments in the Production Plants

	Certain external environment
	Members' data
	Low integrative complexity
	Low tolerance for ambiguity
	Low attitude toward authority (not uncomfortable in strong, controlling authority situations)
	Low attitude toward individualism (prefers to be and work in groups)
	High sense of competence
	Internal environment
High- performing plants	Short-term time orientation
	Strong techno-economic goal orientation

	Influence and control:
	  High formality of structure
	  Perceptions of high structure
	  Perceptions of influence concentrated at top of hierarchy
	  Perceptions of little say, and a more directive supervisory style

	Coordination of work activities:
	  High coordination through high formality of structure
	  Perceptions of high coordination achieved
	  Confrontation mode of conflict resolution in the one plant measured

the internal environment, but rather they were comfortable with well-defined work roles that reserved key decisions for top-level management. Not only did this fit their predispositions, but it matched their views of the external environment they faced.

Finally, members' tendencies to want to work and to be in groups rather than alone fit the higher degree of coordination required by the external environment. A manager in one of the production plants said:

> When I was first made a supervisor in this plant, I listed what I thought my major problems were going to be. I looked at that monster [the multistory, automated production lines] and said one problem was certainly going to be getting people to work together just to keep the lines running. You know,

---

	Certain external environment
	Members' data
	Low integrative complexity
	Low tolerance for ambiguity
	Low attitude toward authority (not uncomfortable in strong, controlling authority situations)
	Low attitude toward individualism (prefers to be and work in groups)
	Low sense of competence
	Internal environment
Low-performing plants	Short-term time orientation
	Weak techno-economic goal orientation

	Influence and control:
	  Low formality of structure
	  Perceptions of low structure
	  Perceptions of more influence exercised at all levels in hierarchy
	  Perceptions of much say, and a less directive, more participatory supervisory style

	Coordination of work activities:
	  Low coordination through low formality of structure
	  Perceptions of low coordination achieved
	  Forcing mode of conflict resolution in the one plant measured

---

that hasn't turned out to be a problem at all for me. The people like to work together here. I won't say that they like that goddamn monster—you'd have to be out of your mind to do that. But they sure do like to work together and that's made one less problem for me as a supervisor.

Thus, the personality dimensions of individuals in all the production plants, regardless of performance levels, were generally well suited to the nature of the external environment and to internal organizational environments with high formality of structure, short-term feedback devices, a hierarchical influence structure, more directive supervision, and highly co-ordinated work patterns. However, only the effective plants had such internal environments. In these effective units, the internal environment simultaneously supported work activities that fit the external environment and individual members' personal predispositions. For the organization, the reward of this three-way fit was high performance. For the individuals in the effective plants, the reward was a sense of competence and mastery. The internal environments of low-performing plants generally had lower formality of structure, more egalitarian influence patterns, more participative supervision, and fewer mechanisms to insure highly coordinated task performance. These factors supported behavior that fit neither the requirements of the external environment nor the members' personality dimensions. We found that this was connected to low performance and low individual feelings of competence in these plants.

Let us end this chapter by returning to the way in which the managers of the effective plants talked about their satisfactions from work. For example, a foreman in the successful container plants:

> My satisfactions come from two things. First, I like the units to run well; I like to see the units run 100 percent of standards. Second, I like to see a mechanical change being of great value. I like to see some *accomplishment*— something *I can see,* something that *others can see,* too. As good as the plant is, I like to see it even better.
>
> The plant's success is due to cooperation—cooperation between supers and between departments. The cooperation is due to the fact that people are *proud of this plant—it's laid out nicely so you can get the job done easily.* It's due to the *enthusiasm* of the people—it's the feeling that "Gee, I like to do this and see that standard met."

Another said:

> What keeps a person coming back and keeps him going is the feeling of prestige and pride in being able to get the job done. It also is the need to seek an increase in status. We influence the attitude of the people on the floor. The attitude we display is reflected in the way the hourly people do their job and how they feel on the job. We've got to realize this more. If the supervisor shows he doesn't care, people will not care. People say, "If the boss doesn't care, why should I?"
>
> There is beautiful coordination among departments here. The people in packing *do* care about us and vice versa. Everyone cares about what kind of container is going out to the customer. The people want to make this plant the best in the company. We work every day to keep the plant on top. Many practices here are geared to help us keep attaining this goal of being the best.
>
> Your job satisfactions come from your overall record. If your costs and output are acceptable to management and then they tell you so, then you can tell your people. Satisfactions come, too, from having brought people along and to have them want to do a job as well as you want. There are more of these kinds of satisfactions than frustrations I have with people.

These comments, like some cited earlier, suggest that these men were very much aware that their feelings about their work were connected to the plant's effectiveness. This supports the notion that one link between unit performance and sense of competence is the feedback that high performance provides the individual about his own competence. But all of the data in this chapter indicate strongly that the three-way fit between personal predispositions, the internal environment, and the external environment also was connected to the relationship between a high sense of competence and effective unit performance, even if organization members were only partially aware of this fact. In Chapter 5 we will determine whether the same relationships were true in the research laboratories.

5

The internal environment
and organization members
within research laboratories

Each of the three pairs of research laboratories was working in a different research area (communications technology; medical technology products; and proprietary drugs), but all dealt with an uncertain external environment where time-span of feedback was long, and where the coordination requirements within the laboratory were relatively low. As mentioned in Chapter 2, one site in each pair had been evaluated by top executives in its parent company as highly effective while the other was regarded as less successful.

From the data in Chapter 3 we know that managers and scientists in all of the laboratories were strikingly alike in the personality predispositions measured. But the data we shall now present indicate that the internal environments of the high-performing laboratories differed substantially from those of the low performers. In presenting these data, we shall explain how such findings are related, not only to differences in performance levels, but also to members' sense of competence, and how these findings—together with the data presented in Chapter 4—support the contingency theory of organizations.

Time and Goal Orientations

Feedback from the external environment about the effectiveness of performance was usually available to the researchers in all the sites only after a relatively long period of work. However, the high tolerance for ambiguity that characterized researchers in all the laboratories meant that they were not uncomfortable with having months or even years pass before they had concrete feedback about the results of their activities. The high-performing laboratories explicitly recognized these factors by holding formal review sessions and reporting on project milestones at less frequent intervals. In the less effective laboratories, reviews and reports of work progress ordinarily occurred more frequently and were seen by scientists as constraining and inconsistent with the long-term nature of their work and with their own personality dimensions. For example, the less successful drug laboratory required written progress reports every two weeks. It also used a screening committee to review weekly the funding of new projects. A researcher in the laboratory commented on the implications of this short-term time frame:

> We're required to write a report on the progress of our research every two weeks. Sometimes there's not much new to talk about. We don't necessarily work on projects that you can make a breakthrough on every two weeks. But, we know we're being evaluated on our reports, so an informal guideline has developed here: The less that's happened since the last report, the longer the current report is. It gets so you rack your brain trying to write a report that makes you look good every two weeks rather than racking your brain to crack open the research problem. That's not my style.

Consistent with these differences in formal practices in the medical products and proprietary drug laboratories, researchers in the more successful sites had a significantly longer time orientation than did members in the less successful sites. As Table 5-1 shows, in the communications laboratories, while the difference in time orientation was in the expected direction, it was not statistically significant. These differences are one factor which seems to explain the dissimilarities in performance and feelings of competence within the various laboratories. A longer-term time orientation meant that the members in the highly effective laboratories were dealing

TABLE 5-1 Members' Time Orientations in the Research Laboratories

Type of laboratory	1 month or less	1-3 months	3-12 months	1-5 years
Effective communications laboratory	0%	5%	17%	78%
Effective medical products laboratory	0	4	27	69
Effective proprietary drug laboratory	3	3	25	69
Less effective communications laboratory	1	5	28	66
Less effective medical laboratory	10	17	46	27
Less effective drug laboratory	15	25	40	20

The percentages refer to the percentage of respondents indicating each category. The categories themselves indicate the amount of time members perceived themselves to be working on problems reaching fruition in the time period specified. The total number of respondents who provided this and all other data about members' own perceptions and experiences of their internal environment was the same as the number of respondents to the tests measuring sense of competence reported in Chapter 3. Converting the percentages above to numbers of respondents in each category results in the following statistical significance of differences in the labs (chi-square distribution):

Communications laboratories	Not significant at the 0.05 level
Medical laboratories	$\chi^2 = 7.23;\ p = < 0.05$
Drug Laboratory	$\chi^2 = 8.94;\ p = < 0.02$

The overall differences between all high-performing laboratories and all low-performing laboratories was significant at the < 0.001 level ($\chi^2 = 16.12$).

more realistically with the long-term feedback which was characteristic of the external environment and which matched their own high tolerance for ambiguity.

Turning to goal orientations, we found that formal practices in the high-performing laboratories encouraged stronger scientific goal orientations than were evident in the low performers. For example, reviews, reports, and evaluations in the effective units emphasized that the ultimate goal of the laboratory was to contribute to the profit and growth of the company by maintaining the laboratory's own identity as a strong *scientific* group interested in influencing operating divisions. A top executive in the effective medical products laboratory said:

> Our performance evaluation criteria and our meetings and review sessions all revolve around industrial research and development goals. We're here to have an effect on operating groups, but we're not willing to lose our own distinctive competencies or expertise in the process. We don't do research and

development in a vacuum, but we sure as hell do do research and development. We do realistic and practical research, but you can bet it's research. We're all scientists "doing science" here. We carry on a dialogue with operating people, not just a monologue—that's how we're evaluated. There's a real communication of ideas so that we and the operating groups can benefit.

In contrast, a researcher in the less effective communications laboratory indicated:

This laboratory is in danger of losing its research image. It's incorporating the goals of marketing and production too much. Management is evaluating us more and more in terms of the sales and dollars we generate. We're starting to lose the distinctive research view. That's a shame, because you need it for checks and balances on sales and the plant.

While elements in the formal practices of all three high-performing laboratories heavily stressed scientific goals, comparable practices in the less effective laboratories placed greater emphasis on some combination of economic, scientific, and marketing goals.

Given these differences in formal practices it is not surprising that members in the high- and low-performing laboratories differed greatly in their actual goal orientations. Professionals in the effective laboratories were more highly concerned with scientific goals than with either economic or marketing goals. As Table 5-2 documents, professionals in the less successful laboratories, although somewhat more concerned with scientific goals than other issues, nonetheless, did not show as high a concern for scientific goals as did the researchers in the more effective sites. In the low-performing laboratories, confusion over goal orientations seemed to be one of the frustrating aspects of the scientists' organizational life. These laboratories were seen as moving heavily toward satisfying plant and marketing conditions and away from the more technically sophisticated research for which their scientists had been trained. One scientist in a low-performing laboratory described some of the outcomes of this shift in emphasis:

We don't do much real research here any more. Fifty percent of us have Ph.D.'s, but we're all working on technically simple projects. Product managers and plant superintendents are getting free advice from Ph.D's. There's not much chance to be creative about research now. The heroic times of research and development have passed here. We're more concerned with profit and loss and with customer acceptance now, whether or not we can be "scientific" in the process. As long as the solutions we give to the simple research problems we work on are believable, everybody's happy. But, that kind of work doesn't allow us to remain technically current. We're not filling in the gaps in our knowledge by giving into sales and plant concerns all the time.

TABLE 5-2 Members' Goal Orientations in the Research Laboratories [a]

Type of laboratory	Scientific	Techno-economic	Marketing
Effective communications laboratory	1.42	2.36	2.21
Effective medical products laboratory	1.43	2.17	2.41
Effective proprietary drug laboratory	1.80	2.08	2.12
Less effective communications laboratory	1.82	2.12	2.07
Less effective medical products laboratory	2.01	1.98	2.01
Less effective drug laboratory	1.90	2.05	2.05

[a] Lower score indicates *more* concern for goal.

The statistical significance in means (all one-tailed probabilities):

	Scientific	Techno-economic	Marketing
Communications laboratories	$t = 5.38; p = < 0.001$	$t = 2.76; p = < 0.01$	$t = 2.65; p = < 0.02$
Medical laboratories	$t = 4.09; p = < 0.001$	$t = 2.45; p = < 0.02$	$t = 2.51; p = < 0.02$
Drug laboratories	$t = 2.33; p = < 0.02$	Not significant at 0.05 level	$t = 2.12; p = < 0.05$

The problem which this researcher raised was not entirely absent from any of the laboratories. Even scientists in high-performing research sites occasionally indicated their frustration over having to do research that, although adequate in terms of production or market, did not always allow the scientists to maintain and expand their scientific expertise. However, based on our interviews and questionnaires, this problem was acute and chronic in the low-performing laboratories, while members of the effective laboratories had goal orientations more consistent with environmental results and their own professional values as scientists. This fit also seems to contribute to their effective performance and their higher feelings of competence.

Formal Control

The effective research laboratories differed from the less effective ones in how precisely defined and controlled were their formal structures (i.e., the extent or absence of formal rules; role definitions; measurement, evaluation, and control systems, etc.) In all three sets of laboratories, the high performers exhibited more flexible and less constraining formal structures and practices than did the lower performing ones. The definition of duties and relationships in all six laboratories was relatively loose, but, in all three sets, the high performer reinforced its flexible job definitions with only a minimum of rules and generalized procedures for performance evaluation and measurement. Lower performers tended to rely on the imposition of more comprehensive rules and procedures and more stringent performance evaluation and control criteria. For example, the less effective medical technology products laboratory had a tightly defined planning and control cycle that did not always make sense in terms of the uncertainty of the external environment or the members' high tolerance for ambiguity and high integrative complexity. One professional there said:

> This laboratory operates by the book on rules and controls. Everything is by the numbers, even on things like making out travel vouchers. Its bing-bing-bing all the way down the line. It was looser in manufacturing when I was working there. Tight controls mean that I fill in the same reports the same way, day in and day out. My job changes so much that the information I supply is often irrelevant, or, even worse, redundant.

In contrast, a scientist in the high-performing medical products laboratory joked that: "We can't wear sandals because of safety regulations and we're not supposed to proposition secretaries on company time, but apart from that there's not much formality in the laboratory."

Additionally, both the lower-performing communications and drug laboratories emphasized written rules about arriving for work on time, taking coffee breaks, using company telephone lines, etc., to a greater extent than did their successful counterparts. Commenting on the rigidity of these rules, one researcher in a low-performing lab indicated:

> There's a strict rule about getting here on time. No one rewards you for staying late in the department, but you have to sign in in the morning to insure you're here on time. . . . What you get is scientists coming in precisely at 8:00 A.M. but then leaving precisely at 4:30 no matter where they are on their project. If you want to see a guy after 4:30 around here, you'd better make an appointment or he'll be gone.

In the high-performing labs it was a general norm to come and go at one's own discretion. Scientists typically came in at odd hours of the day, stayed long after "regular" working hours, took breaks when their work allowed, and even came in on weekends. An executive in a high-performing laboratory was quick to note:

Because we don't have many rules here doesn't mean we're lax. There is a thing going on in this lab that's evident the first day you're here. *People discipline themselves.* There's no need for rules. We're supposed to put in 39 hours a week, but I don't know one person in the lab who does—it's always more than that, and it's always based on the requirements of the project you're working on. We come and go as our work requires. That's the way you should treat professionals.

This executive highlighted important differences in assumptions on the part of top administrators in the high- and low-performing sites. Managers in the high performers tended to rely on researchers' self-discipline and self-control, while managers in the lower performers assumed the need for more pervasive rules and other formal devices in the internal environment to control members' work activities. Essentially, in the high-performing laboratories there was more reliance on the personal standards which members had developed as professional scientists, whereas in the low performers there was more reliance on formally imposed controls. This point was borne out by our interviews with laboratory and company executives and by our investigation of formal documents and manuals in each laboratory. From data on formal structure and practices which appears in Sections 1, 2, and 3 of the "Researcher's Data Sheet for Unit Formal Practices," in the "Methodological Appendix," we were able to position the laboratories on the grid in Figure 5-1, rating them from low to high formality of structure. Only where the formal organization of the laboratory matched both the external environment and members' predispositions was there high-system performance and the intrinsic reward of a strong sense of competence.

Practices in the high performers seemed to be more consistent with the uncertainty of the external environment because information about how to solve research problems and make decisions was changing rapidly and activities could not be rigidly defined in advance. This interpretation is supported by Pelz and Andrews who found that researchers in scientific organizations which did not define many formal rules or place controls on research activities tended to perform their work more effectively than did those in tightly controlling organizations.[1] Self-discipline and self-control also seemed more consistent with the high integrative complexity and high tolerance for ambiguity that researchers generally showed, along with their desire to work without dependence on authority figures. Researchers preferred to develop their own means of sensing and responding to external en-

[1] Donald C. Pelz and Frank M. Andrews, *Scientists in Organizations: Productive Climates for Research and Development* (New York: Wiley, 1966).

Fig. 5-1. The formal structure in the research laboratories.[a]

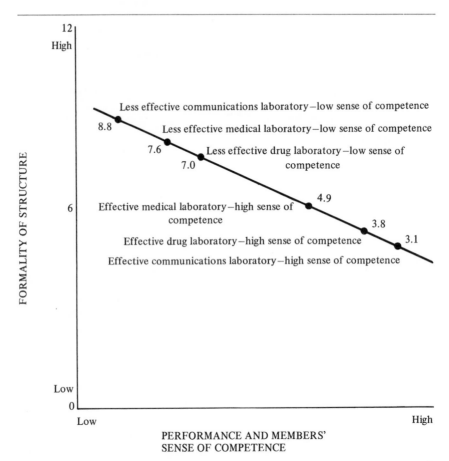

[a] Average scores for Sections 1, 2, and 3 of the "Researcher's Data Sheet for Unit Formal Practices" were added together to position a laboratory on the grid.

vironment information and could process that information at a high level of complexity without having to rely on organization rules for its processing. They were also quite comfortable in settings that were ill-defined, unclear, and ambiguous. Similarly, they preferred to work autonomously without direction from superiors. Managers in the high-performing laboratories recognized the members' personality predispositions and the requirements of the uncertain external environment by relying on the self-discipline of their researchers rather than utilizing a highly formal structure.[2] Apparently, the risks of allowing this degree of autonomy were not high, because the scientists were strongly guided by their professional standards and interests and their desire to feel competent to act in ways which met the units' goals.

Members' perceptions of the influence and control pattern

In the light of the discussion above and as Fig. 5-2 shows, it is not un-expected that members in the high-performing laboratories *perceived* less formality of structure in their unit's internal environment than did members in the less effective labs. This meant that professionals in the success-ful site perceived that they could behave flexibly and adaptively, consistent with the rapidly changing information in the external environment and with their own high levels of integrative complexity, tolerance for ambiguity, and their preference for autonomy from authority. In the less effective sites, professionals saw their work activities as more controlled and well defined and, therefore, less suited to their predispositions and the external environ-ments. One scientist in the less effective medical technology products laboratory indicated:

> There's something in this laboratory that keeps you from being scientific. It's hard to put your finger on, but I guess I'd call it "Mickey Mouse." There are rules and things here that get in your way regarding doing your job as a researcher. There is a preponderance of little things that have to be done, but that take you away from your work. I spend too much time on trivia. . . . It doesn't leave much time to sink your teeth into your research. I guess it gets back to my point on trivia. This lab sometimes feels it's doing a good job because of the amount of paper work we generate. We confuse activity with creative accomplishment.

In contrast, a researcher in the effective medical products lab, when asked about the absence of formal rules, commented:

> If a man puts a nut on a screw all day long, you may need more rules and job definition for him. We're not novices here. We're professionals and not the kind who need close supervision. People around here do produce, and produce under relaxed conditions. I couldn't do my job with lots of rules and procedures. They would get in my way, jobwise and personally.

The highly effective research labs also had more total influence being exercised by their members. Similarly, influence in the successful labora-

---

[2] George F. Farris, in "Organizational Factors and Individual Performance: A Longitudinal Study," *Journal of Applied Psychology* 53 (April 1969):87-92, argues that causality may go in the opposite direction. That is, as scientists and researchers perform better, they are given more freedom and autonomy. This point does not appear inconsistent with our position and findings.

Fig. 5-2. Members' perceptions of the degree of structure in the laboratories.

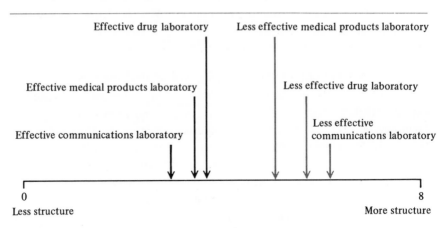

Scores for the members' perceptions of degree of structure were obtained by combining scores for the perceptions of (1) behavioral conformity and (2) organizational clarity in the laboratories. Laboratory scores are indicated below. Lower score indicates perceptions of less structure.

	Conformity	Clarity	Total structure
Effective communications laboratory	1.78	2.22	4.00
Effective medical products laboratory	2.02	2.16	4.18
Effective drug laboratory	1.98	2.64	4.62
Less effective medical products laboratory	2.63	2.68	5.31
Less effective drug laboratory	2.42	2.96	5.38
Less effective communications laboratory	2.73	3.34	6.07

The statistical significance of difference in means (all one-tailed probabilities):

	Conformity	Clarity	Total structure
Communications laboratories	$t = 9.84;\ p = < 0.001$	$t = 9.17;\ p = < 0.001$	$t = 12.13;\ p = < 0.001$
Medical laboratories	$t = 4.74;\ p = < 0.001$	$t = 3.16;\ p = < 0.01$	$t = 5.49;\ p = < 0.001$
Drug laboratories	$t = 3.20;\ p = < 0.01$	$t = 1.95;\ p = < 0.05$	$t = 3.67;\ p = < 0.001$

tories was present throughout many levels of the organizational hierarchy. As Figs. 5-3 and 5-4 indicate, less effective labs had lower total influence, which was perceived to be more concentrated in the upper levels of the hierarchy. Greater total influence in the more effective sites meant that researchers were more heavily involved in decisions concerning the defini-

Fig. 5-3. Amount of influence in the laboratories.

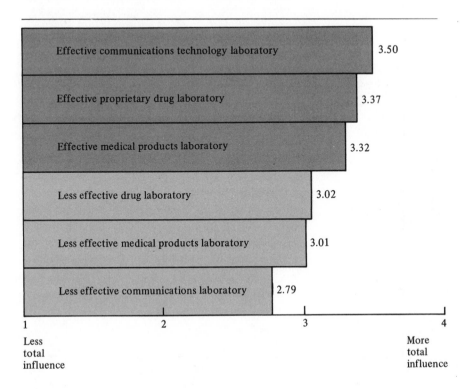

Effective communications technology laboratory   3.50

Effective proprietary drug laboratory   3.37

Effective medical products laboratory   3.32

Less effective drug laboratory   3.02

Less effective medical products laboratory   3.01

Less effective communications laboratory   2.79

1   2   3   4

Less total influence   More total influence

Scores reported are the means for each laboratory. Higher scores indicate perceptions of higher total influence exercised in the laboratory. The statistical significance of difference in means (all one-tailed probabilities):

Communications laboratories	$t = 2.49$; $p = <0.02$
Medical laboratories	$t = 2.58$; $p = <0.02$
Drug laboratories	$t = 2.54$; $p = <0.02$

tion and performance of their work activities. They saw themselves and their colleagues having a great deal of influence over work activities, more so than did researchers in the less effective laboratories. Members of the successful sites also saw decision-making influence broadly spread across many levels, while scientists in the less successful sites perceived influence to be more concentrated in upper-managerial levels.

In general, decision-making ought to be centered in the organizational

Fig. 5-4. Distribution of influence in the laboratories.

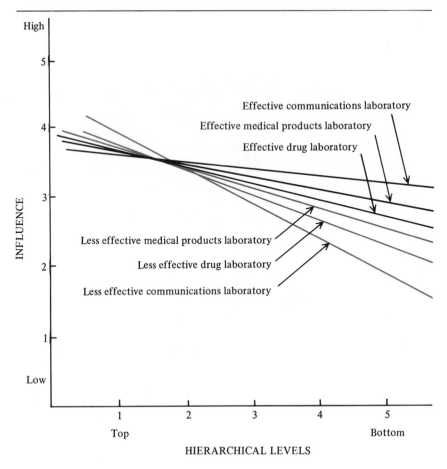

Lines fitted by least squares method, with the model $Y=BX+A$. Regression equations for each line were:

Highly effective communications laboratory	$Y = -0.07X + 3.75$
Highly effective medical products laboratory	$Y = -0.18X + 3.85$
Highly effective proprietary drug laboratory	$Y = -0.30X + 3.99$
Less effective medical products laboratory	$Y = -0.39X + 3.97$
Less effective proprietary drug laboratory	$Y = -0.44X + 4.10$
Less effective communications laboratory	$Y = -0.66X + 4.59$

The statistical significance of difference in slopes (one-tailed probabilities):

Communications laboratories	$t = 47.52; p = < 0.001$
Medical laboratories	$t = 17.85; p = < 0.001$
Drug laboratories	$t = 9.78; p = < 0.001$

The steeper the line, the more hierarchical the distribution of influence. The flatter the line, the more egalitarian the distribution of influence.

levels where knowledge to make the decisions is available.[3] Knowledge to make decisions in this uncertain external environment very often resided with the scientist working on the bench (the lowest professional level in the laboratories). The high-performing laboratories provided such scientists with more influence in the internal environment than did the less effective units. Equally important, the researchers, because of their high integrative complexity and attitude toward authority, preferred freedom and autonomy on the job to solve complex problems on their own and would be uncomfortable in strong, controlling authority relationships where much of the decision-making influence rested with superiors. A scientist in a less successful lab posed this dilemma:

> Management pretty much sets parameters on the research projects for us, especially around time and budget commitments. I rarely get involved, even when I ask to. But, I have information that could be valuable in setting the terms of the project. That information could make the constraints on the project more "liveable," but it's not used. I want to be brought in on more decisions. I also have needed information.

This can be contrasted with the view of a manager in a highly successful medical laboratory who indicated that a critical dimension of the external environment was that no one manager in a laboratory could handle all the complicated kinds of information necessary to perform well. Consequently, managers had to rely on others in the laboratories for such knowledge. The manager commented:

> I don't have the expert knowledge about radiology that even one of our newest scientists has. It would be plain foolish for me to try to second-guess him in that field. So, we expect everyone in the lab to help decide the things we do. I run my meetings with research personnel so that each one knows he has an equal voice in the major decisions we make. You can't run a place any other way with as many different kinds of knowledge represented as we have here and with the kind of people that we have here who have to be brought in on major decisions.

"Say" and supervisory style

Other indications of members' influence and control over work activities came from their perceptions of how much "say" they had in choosing and handling research projects and their perceptions of the typical supervisory style in their unit. As Table 5-3 shows, high- and low-performing laboratories did not differ much in the say researchers felt they had in handling a

---

[3] Paul R. Lawrence and Jay W. Lorsch, *Organization and Environment* (Boston: Harvard Business School, Division of Research, 1967) pp. 71-73.

project on their own. Generally, all laboratories gave members a free rein in carrying out the complexities of a research project, subject, of course, to the time and budget constraints imposed by the project. High and low performers did differ markedly, though, in the amount of say researchers felt they had in initially selecting the project on which they were to work. In high-performing laboratories more than in low-performing ones, researchers

TABLE 5-3 Freedom and Autonomy to Choose and Handle Work Activities in the Laboratories

	"Say" in handling task on own once chosen		
	High	Medium	Low
Effective communications laboratory	78%	22%	0%
Effective medical products laboratory	80	20	0
Effective proprietary drug laboratory	67	28	5
Less effective communications laboratory	67	28	5
Less effective medical products laboratory	64	30	6
Less effective drug laboratory	50	42	8

The percentages again refer to the percentage of respondents indicating each category. Based on a chi-square distribution, none of the differences between each pair of laboratories were significant at the 0.05 level, but the overall differences between all high-performing laboratories and all low-performing laboratories was significant at the < 0.05 level ($\chi^2 = 6.71$).

	"Say" in initially choosing own tasks		
	High	Medium	Low
Effective communications laboratory	59%	37%	4%
Effective medical products laboratory	60	40	0
Effective proprietary drug laboratory	33	50	17
Less effective communications laboratory	24	57	19
Less effective medical products laboratory	17	30	54
Less effective drug laboratory	14	50	36

The percentages refer to the percentage of respondents indicating each category. The total number of respondents in each laboratory was the same as the number of respondents to the tests measuring sense of competence reported in Chapter 3. Converting the percentages to numbers of respondents in each category results in the following statistical significance of differences in the laboratories (chi-square distribution):

Communcations laboratories	$\chi^2 = 6.06; \ p = < 0.02$
Medical laboratories	$\chi^2 = 15.25; \ p = < 0.001$
Drug laboratories	$\chi^2 = 4.65; \ p = < 0.05$

were heavily involved in the selection of projects and in the setting of performance parameters and milestones. These data suggest that such professionals perceived themselves to have more freedom and autonomy in influencing the specific decisions affecting the direction of their work. This could result in a researcher using his particular area of expertise and technical competence to select projects with a higher probability of technical success than would be possible if top management monopolized the project decisions. The greater say in decision-making in the effective laboratories would also appeal to members with a high tolerance for ambiguity in decision-making, as well as to members who, because of their attitude toward authority, would be uncomfortable where superiors made most of the decisions.

With regard to supervisory style, we believed, a priori, that in an uncertain external environment, participative supervision would be more appropriate than either a directive or a laissez-faire style. Also, the laboratories in our study, as indicated in Chapter 2, focused on the development of products and technology for transfer to operating groups. Top managers and supervisors tended to have more information about business and profit goals than did researchers, but researchers tended to have more technical information and expertise in specific research disciplines than did higher-level supervisors. The sharing of both kinds of information through a participative style of supervision should lead to more realistic decisions and higher performance, and should make sense to people whose attitude toward authority makes them uncomfortable with decisions coming mostly from above. As Table 5-4 indicates, high-performing laboratories, more so than low performers, did have internal environments in which the participatory style of supervision that fit the nature of the information in the external environment and members' own personality dimensions was more typical. Less successful labs relied more on laissez-faire and/or directive supervision. This meant that in the low-performing laboratories one of the two critical information inputs identified above was missing from the decision-making process and that members who preferred autonomy were in internal environments that did not match their personal preferences. This reinforces our explanation of differences in effectiveness and, simultaneously, members' own feelings of competence in the laboratories. A manager in the successful drug laboratory, while commenting on the quality of decisions in his unit, offered an additional reason why participatory supervision worked well:

Researchers need pressure to be creative, especially when they're working in industrial research. But this pressure can't be phony. It's got to come from the commitment of the researcher himself. You have to be open and share information and decision-making responsibility or nothing will happen to create the pressure. I'm not that interested in saving face. . . . I don't have to make all the decisions. . . . I don't have all the information needed to make good ones. There are few unilateral decisions made here. I want the researchers involved. If you can set up an environment of commitment by being open, trusting, sharing information, and having all your people involved in decisions, the pressure to be creative results almost automatically. There are no devices to get that pressure for creativity. It's an environment that's part of this lab. There's a high element of personal dedication and commitment to creative decisions here.

Thus, sharing information and decision-making responsibility through participatory supervision may be related, not only to more realistic research decisions and the researchers' own attitudes toward authority, but also to more personal commitment to a norm of creativity and innovation on the part of the scientists.

While some behavioral scientists argue that a high degree of participatory supervision, mutual decision-making, and shared information are equally appropriate to all organizational units and all external environments, the data from this study suggest that the type of supervision ought to be conditional on the requirements of the external environment facing the organi-

TABLE 5-4 Type of Supervision in the Laboratories

Type of laboratory	Participative	Directive	Laissez-faire
Effective communications laboratory	74%	13%	13%
Effective medical products laboratory	70	10	20
Effective proprietary drug laboratory	72	17	11
Less effective communications laboratory	52	19	29
Less effective medical products laboratory	41	18	41
Less effective drug laboratory	50	23	27

The percentages again refer to the percentage of respondents indicating each category. The statistical significance of differences in number of respondents in each pair of laboratories (chi-square distribution):

Communications laboratories	$\chi^2 = 5.72$; $p = < 0.05$
Medical laboratories	$\chi^2 = 6.86$; $p = < 0.05$
Drug laboratories	$\chi^2 = 6.25$; $p = < 0.05$

zation and on members' own attitudes toward authority.[4] The work requirements and people's predispositions around a relatively certain external environment (as in the production plants surveyed in Chapter 4) suggest the need for more emphasis on a directive type of supervision, although some participation is also appropriate. In contrast, the work requirements and people's predispositions in a relatively uncertain external environment (as in the laboratories studied here) call for a highly participatory style.

It also is worth emphasizing at this juncture, that while the thrust of our argument is that a participatory style seems to lead to effective performance, given the predispositions of members and the nature of the external environment, the causality is not necessarily all in this direction. For example, it may well be that low performance in the laboratory in prior time periods has led top management to become more directive. Thus, feedback about performance is an active agent in the system. Nevertheless, such emphasis on managerial direction seems to have been counterproductive for the low-performing laboratories.

Coordination of work activities

There was not much need for researchers in these laboratories to coordinate or integrate their individualized projects in order to attain the overall goals of the laboratories. Because a scientist typically worked on his own projects in his own specialized areas of expertise, he ordinarily did not relate his work activities much with the activities of other researchers. Only high-performing laboratories had the low degree of formality of structure that left researchers free to tackle individualized projects, unencumbered by unnecessary formal devices for coordination and control. The internal environments of the less effective laboratories, as we noted earlier, contained more formal rules and procedures for coordination and control. This probably imposed more requirements for coordination among researchers than were appropriate to the successful performance of the diverse research projects. Equally important, since researchers generally indicated predispositions for being and working alone, internal organizational environments that stressed formal coordination and many integrative devices would not make much sense to their members. We were not surprised when, as Table

[4] See, for example, Chris Argyris, *Integrating the Individual and the Organization* (New York: Wiley, 1964); Rensis Likert, *The Human Organization: Its Management and Value* (New York: McGraw-Hill, 1967); and William J. Roche and Neil L. MacKinnon, "Motivating People with Meaningful Work," *Harvard Business Review* 48 (May-June 1970):97:110.

5-5 shows, the members in two of the high-performing sites perceived a significantly lower degree of coordination of work effort among colleagues than did their counterparts in the less effective labs. The difference in the third pair of laboratories (medical products) was not statistically significant, but was in the predicted direction.

It is important to emphasize here that lower coordination of work activities in the high-performing laboratories in no way meant fewer interactions among colleagues for sharing new knowledge and testing the feasibility of ideas and concepts. Scientists used each other regularly for evaluating and analyzing their ideas and research approaches. Even though the researchers may have been working on different projects in different fields, they relied heavily on each other to provide a critical sounding board for new thoughts. We observed small groups of scientists in ad hoc problem-solving interactions both during and after normal working hours. In fact, a researcher in the highly successful communications laboratory noted:

> Each office in this building is a miniature conference room. There's not a day goes by that a couple of fellows don't drop by my place to mess up my blackboard with their equations. And there's not a day goes by that I don't moonlight in somebody else's office messing up his blackboard with my equations.

Clearly, because the professionals in the high-performing laboratories were

TABLE 5-5 Coordination of Work Activities in the Research Laboratories

Type of laboratory	Low	Medium	High
Effective communications laboratory	27%	46%	27%
Effective medical products laboratory	40	40	20
Effective proprietary drug laboratory	33	50	17
Less effective communications laboratory	5	24	71
Less effective medical products laboratory	35	35	30
Less effective drug laboratory	9	36	55

The percentages refer to the percentage of respondents indicating each category. The statistical significance of differences in number of respondents in each pair of laboratories (chi-square distribution):

Communications laboratories	$\chi^2 = 10.35; p = < 0.01$
Medical laboratories	Not significant at the 0.05 level
Drug laboratories	$\chi^2 = 6.94; p = < 0.05$

The overall differences between all high-performing laboratories and all low-performing laboratories were significant at the <0.001 level, ($\chi^2 = 15.62$).

not required to heavily integrate their individualistic work activities and because they may have preferred to work alone did not mean that they did not interact and communicate with each other to solve technical problems. Indeed, it may have been that the absence of externally imposed coordination requirements in the high performers may have encouraged vital ad hoc colleague interaction when the individuals felt it was necessary to solve rapidly changing problems.

Members in both the effective and less successful laboratories also behaved differently in resolving conflicts. As Table 5-6 shows, the dominant mode was confrontation in each of the three successful laboratories. Only one of the less effective laboratories (the less successful medical technology products laboratory) used confrontation as its dominant mode. But, even here, the members of the more effective medical laboratory confronted conflict significantly more often than did members of its sister site. The other two low-performing laboratories relied primarily on the forcing mode. Con-

TABLE 5-6 Modes of Conflict Resolution in the Research Laboratories [a]

Type of laboratory	Confrontation	Forcing	Smoothing
Effective communications laboratory	2.01 [b]	2.88	3.16
Effective medical products laboratory	2.26 [b]	2.93	3.25
Effective proprietary drug laboratory	2.28 [b]	3.04	3.32
Less effective communications laboratory	2.55	2.29 [b]	3.35
Less effective medical products laboratory	2.60 [b]	2.84	3.34
Less effective drug laboratory	2.52	2.32 [b]	3.27

[a] Lower score indicates *more* use of mode.
[b] Dominant mode of conflict resolution in the laboratory, that is, the behavior most typically used to solve problems and achieve coordination.

The statistical significance of difference in means (all one-tailed probabilities):

	Confrontation	Forcing	Smoothing
Communications laboratories	$t = 5.99$; $p_j = < 0.001$	$t = 3.86$; $p = < 0.001$	None of the differences
Medical laboratories	$t = 2.32$; $p = < 0.02$	$t = 2.54$; $p = < 0.02$	here were significant
Drug laboratories	$t = 2.82$; $p = < 0.01$	$t = 4.21$; $p = < 0.001$	at the 0.05 level

fronting problems to find the basis for disagreement, as well as the basis for potential agreement, as the researchers in the three successful labs most often did, meant the problems were resolved in terms of the underlying causes. Thus, the researchers were able to turn their attention and energies to other emerging issues in the rapidly changing and uncertain external environment. Forcing solutions, which researchers in two of the less successful labs indicated was their most typical behavior, meant that solutions there were likely to be based on the will of the most powerful party, and not on the basis of all the available information. We should point out that the confrontation mode of conflict resolution utilized in the high-performing labs seemed to be less directly related to the uncertainty of the external environment or to the personality dimensions of members than it was to the desire among individuals to get on with the job and to perform it well.

Differences in the Internal Environments of the Research Laboratories

Our findings about the differences in member characteristics and in the internal environments of the high- and low-performing research laboratories are shown in Table 5-7. As in Chapter 4, we must consider a three-way fit among members' predispositions, the external environment, and the characteristics of the internal environment in order to fully understand the effectiveness of unit performance and the strength of members' feelings of competence.

Because of the personality makeup of the members in all the research laboratories, they were well suited to the unpredictability and uncertainty of the external environment and to internal environments with low formality of structure, long-term feedback mechanisms, widely shared influence processes, more participatory supervision, and low coordination of work activities. However, only the high-performing laboratories had internal environments which fit members' predispositions and the uncertainty of the external environment. Individuals in the high-performing laboratories could behave in ways which were consistent with their predispositions and with the uncertainty of the external environment, precisely because the internal environment also fit both sets of variables. The result was high unit performance and, for members, the reward of strong feelings of competency. The internal environments of low-performing laboratories, with greater formality of structure, less widely diffused decision-making influence, more directive supervision, and greater coordination of work activities, fit the external

TABLE 5-7 The Findings About Members' Characteristics and Internal Organization Environments in the Research Laboratories

	Uncertain external environment

High-performing research laboratories	*Members' data*
	High integrative complexity
	High tolerance for ambiguity
	High on attitude toward authority
	   (prefers independence and autonomy)
	High on attitude toward individualism
	   (prefers to be and work alone)
	High sense of competence
	
	Internal environment
	Long-term time orientation
	Strong scientific goal orientation
	Influence and control:
	   Low formality of structure
	   Perceptions of low structure
	   Perceptions of much influence widely diffused throughout the
	     laboratory
	   Perceptions of much "say" and a participative style of supervision
	Coordination of work activities:
	   Low coordination through low formality of structure
	   Perceptions of low coordination required and achieved
	   Confrontation mode of conflict resolution

Low-performing research laboratories	*Members' data*
	High integrative complexity
	High tolerance for ambiguity
	High on attitude toward authority
	   (prefers independence and autonomy)
	High on attitude toward individualism
	   (prefers to be and work alone)
	Low sense of competence
	
	Internal enivronment
	Shorter-term time orientation
	Weak scientific goal orientation
	Influence and control:
	   High formality of structure
	   Perceptions of high structure
	   Perceptions of influence concentrated at top of hierarchy
	   Perceptions of little "say" and a directive style of supervision
	Coordination of work activities:
	   High coordination through high formality of structure
	   Perceptions of high coordination of activities
	   More forcing mode of conflict resolution

environment less well. Further, in the lower-performing laboratories, the internal environment promoted work behavior that was inappropriate to the personality preferences of members. Our findings suggest that these mismatches were related to the lower unit performance and lower individual feelings of competence from work.

It is easy to slip into an interpretation of the data in this chapter which suggests that low-performing laboratories will always have structures which are too high, influence patterns which are too hierarchical, etc. However, this is not the way we believe these data should be analyzed. Rather, we feel the appropriate conclusion, as suggested above, is that the high performers had a more appropriate fit between internal environmental characteristics, external environmental requirements, and members' predispositions than did the low performers. While, for example, the low performers we studied all tended to err in the direction of too great a formality of struc-

Fig. 5-5. Example of actual and possible mismatch in formality of structure of research laboratories.

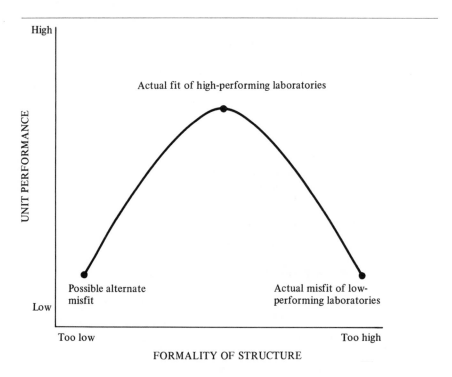

UNIT PERFORMANCE

High

Actual fit of high-performing laboratories

Possible alternate misfit

Actual misfit of low-performing laboratories

Low

Too low

Too high

FORMALITY OF STRUCTURE

ture, it is theoretically possible that they might have erred in the direction of too little structure, as Fig. 5-5 demonstrates. Our reason for stressing this point is to make it clear that we do not feel that units need to be high or low on any particular element of the internal environment, but rather that each unit's internal environment must achieve an appropriate fit with its members and its external environment, and that a mismatch is theoretically possible in either a high or low direction.

One possible reason that all the low research performers in this study erred in the same direction can be found in Lawrence and Lorsch's findings about differentiation among functional units.[5] Since, according to their findings, research laboratories usually tend to be the least formalized units in an organization, it may very well be that managers who are having performance problems with a laboratory tend to make it more like the other units in the organization. Thus, they increase the formality of structure. This not only meets the commonly held management assumption that when a unit is not working well tighter control is a good remedy, but also tends to reduce differentiation between the research laboratories and other units, which might make integration among these units seem easier to achieve.

In Chapters 4 and 5 we have studied the differences between high- and low-performing sites within each type of external environment. In Chapter 6 we shall draw together all of these data by comparing the high- and low-performing units in both external environments. Additionally, we shall consider the practical administrative implications of this study, as well as its contribution to the contingency theory of organizations.

[5] Lawrence and Lorsch, *Organization*.

Contingency theory and administration

Summary and Interpretation of Findings

The major question which this study has sought to answer is whether a fit among the internal environment, the external environment, and the predisposition of members is related to effective unit performance, as well as to rewards for individual members in terms of their feelings of competence. When the total pattern of these data is viewed as a whole, as it is in Table 6-1, the answer to this question clearly is in the affirmative.

In the effective units within the two external environments studied, members experienced a strong sense of competence from very different kinds of work activities which, in turn, were supported by dissimilar kinds of internal environments. Likewise, the individuals working within the two external environments preferred different kinds of activities because of differences in their personal predispositions. When these three sets of variables—*the external environment, the internal environment, and members' personality dimensions*—were congruent with each other, units in both kinds of external

TABLE 6-1 Members' Data and Internal Organizational Environments in Manufacturing and Research External Environment

	Certainty of external environment
High	**Low**
Members' data	*Members' data*
Low integrative complexity	High integrative complexity
Low tolerance for ambiguity	High tolerance for ambiguity
Low on attitude toward authority (not uncomfortable in strong, controlling authority relations)	High on attitude toward authority (prefers freedom and autonomy in authority relations)
Low on attitude toward individualism (prefers to be and work in groups)	High on attitude toward individualism (prefers to be and work alone)
High sense of competence	High sense of competence
Internal environment	*Internal environment*
Short-term time orientation	Long-term time orientation
Strong techno-economic goal orientation	Strong scientific goal orientation
Influence and control:	Influence and control:
High formality of structure	Low formality of structure
Perceptions of high structure	Perceptions of low structure
Perceptions of influence concentrated at top of hierarchy	Perceptions of much influence diffused throughout many levels of hierarchy
Perceptions of little "say" and directive supervision	Perceptions of much "say" and participatory supervision
Coordination of work activities:	Coordination of work activities:
High coordination through high formality of structure	Low coordination through low formality of structure
Perceptions of high coordination achieved	Perceptions of low coordination required and achieved
Confrontation mode of conflict resolution	Confrontation mode of conflict resolution

UNIT'S PERFORMANCE—HIGH

environment were successful and individuals were rewarded by stronger feelings of competence.

On the other hand, in the less effective units within both external environments, members did not feel such a strong sense of competence. In their personality tendencies, however, they were quite similar to their counterparts in the successful sites within the same external environment. Even though a match existed between members' personalities and the external environment in all of the low performers, the important point is that the

Certainty of external environment	
High	*Low*
Members' data	**Members' data**
Low integrative complexity	High integrative complexity
Low tolerance for ambiguity	High tolerance for ambiguity
Low on attitude toward authority (not uncomfortable in strong, controlling authority relations)	High on attitude toward authority (prefers freedom and autonomy in authority relations)
Low on attitude toward individualism (prefers to be and work in groups)	High on attitude toward individualism (prefers to be and work alone)
Low sense of competence	Low sense of competence
Internal environment	**Internal environment**
Short-term time orientation	Short-term time orientation
Weak techno-economic goal orientation	Weak scientific goal orientation
Influence and control:	Influence and control:
Low formality of structure	High formality of structure
Perceptions of low structure	Perceptions of high structure
Perceptions of much influence exercised at all hierarchy levels	Perceptions of low influence, concentrated at top levels
Perceptions of much "say" and less directive, more participatory supervision	Perceptions of little "say" and directive and/or laissez-faire supervision
Coordination of work activities:	Coordination of work activities:
Low coordination through low formality of structure	High coordination through high formality of structure
Perceptions of low coordination achieved	Perceptions of high coordination achieved
Forcing mode of conflict resolution	Forcing mode of conflict resolution

(Left margin, vertical: UNIT'S PERFORMANCE—LOW)

internal environments of the less effective units suited neither the requirements of the external environment nor members' predispositions. This incongruence in both kinds of external environment was associated with less successful unit operations and less reward for individuals from a sense of competence. All these data underscore that effective unit performance and members' individual feelings of competence are found only when a three-way match among member characteristics, the unit's internal environment, and its external environment is also present.

Having established that this set of relationships exists, we are still left with the question of causality. Earlier we suggested three possible reasons for the association between unit performance and an individual member's feelings of competence:

1. Members of the high-performing units had greater feelings of competence before they joined these units, and their feelings were sustained.
2. The high performance of the effective units provided feedback to individual members which enhanced their feelings of competence.
3. The three-way fit among members' predispositions and internal and external environmental factors led to high performance of the unit and to its members feeling more competent.

Apropos of the first explanation, our research was not designed to test it explicitly; however, there is nothing in our data to lead us to refute it. Concerning the second possible explanation, much of the interview data cited in the prior chapters clearly support it. Individuals indicated that their effectiveness on the job was leading them to feel more competent. Finally, the total pattern of our data does strongly support the third, or *fit*, explanation. Thus, we have support for at least two of these explanations. This is consistent with the view taken in Chapter 3 that they were not necessarily mutually exclusive and leads us to conclude that the conceptual view of the relationships which we posited in Chapter 1 is consistent with the total pattern of our data.

Figure 6-1 highlights the fact that the relationship between man and the internal and external environments of his work organization seems to be a highly complex and contingent one. When there is a fit among the internal and external environments of the unit and members' predispositions, unit members are more effective in processing information and reaching and implementing their decisions. This would seem to be an important force in producing the effective results which existed in the high-performing units (see relationship 1 in Fig. 6-1). The fact that the fit enables the individual to act effectively leads him to feel more competent (see relationship 2). But the performance results themselves also provide feedback to individuals and enhance their feelings of competence (see relationship 3). This is not necessarily the end of the cycle, however, and it is for this reason that the arrows in Fig. 6-1 are two-directional. The unit's effective performance provides feedback to management and members which encourages them to maintain the fit (see relationship 4). In addition, the desirability of maintaining the present fit is also reinforced because each member wishes to

Fig. 6-1. An overview of relationships between individual and organizations.

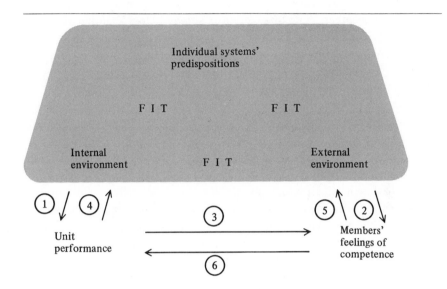

continue his feeling of competence (see relationship 5). Finally, the fact that individuals feel competent encourages them to continue to strive for effective performance (see relationship 6).

In the low-performing units, the dynamics would appear to be similar, but with a reverse effect. In these situations, the *lack* of fit leads members to be less able to accomplish their work effectively. Both because of their inability to act effectively and because of feedback about low performance, members feel less competent. This, in turn, reduces their incentive to perform the work required. It also may make members and their top managers more willing to consider changes in the existing mismatch between environmental factors and individual predispositions, but in the lower-performing units studied there was no evidence that top management understood what action might be appropriate for solving their problems. Our findings, however, clearly suggest the direction in which such action should be taken for low-performing units, and that is toward the fit which existed in the comparable more effective units. Shortly we shall fully explore the implications of this study for managerial action, but before doing so it is important to explore more carefully the fit between individual predispositions and the unit's external and internal environments.

So far, the implicit argument has been made that a fit between internal environmental characteristics and members' predispositions is important because the members had these predispositions before entering the unit. This is consistent with the view of the individual mentioned at the outset: that his predispositions are a function of his biological makeup and the process of socialization from birth through adulthood. An alternative interpretation of our findings about members' predispositions is that somehow the differences among individuals could best be explained as the result of socialization into different internal organizational cultures. This latter position would be hard to support on two grounds. First, the participants in the study were selected to represent people who had been with the organization for both short and long terms. Second, and more important, differences in predispositions along our four dimensions did not exist either between members of the high- and low-performing laboratories or between members of the high- and low-performing plants. If a socialization or acculturation process were having an effect on an individual because of his working in a particular internal environment, we would expect a systematic and consistent difference among individuals which would be related to differences in the internal environmental elements described in the preceding chapters. This would mean that, because of differences in the units' internal environments, members of the high-performing laboratories should be different from those of the less effective labs in the four personality predispositions measured, while members of the more effective plants should be different from those of the lower-performing plants. Our findings indicate that such differences simply did not exist.

One other possible explanation of these findings is that they reflect differences in the location of the sites and the related cultural effects of individuals living in different sections of the United States. For example, Hulin and Blood, in their view of job-enlargement literature, suggest that ideas about the relationship between job size and job satisfaction should be modified to take into account the impact of the location of the plant and the cultural backgrounds of the workers.[1] To the extent that the location of the organization and the cultural background of its members meant that individuals might have different biological makeups and different patterns of experience in personality development, we would support these views as

[1] Charles L. Hulin and Milton R. Blood, "Job Enlargement, Individual Differences and Worker Responses," *Psychological Bulletin* 69 (1968):41-55.

being consistent with our ideas about the nature of the individual's system. But our sites were widely scattered around the country and were in both urban and rural areas. Further, the managerial and professional personnel who were the subject of this study tended to be highly mobile, making it unlikely that the personnel in any one site were drawn solely from the immediate locale. All of this leads us to conclude that there was no systematic impact of organization location in the study.

Having put these two alternative explanations aside, we must conclude that the fit between the individual's predispositions and the unit's external and internal environments is related to both unit performance and the individual's feelings of competence through the complex set of relationships outlined above. Thus, our data have enabled us to begin to understand how the nature of the unit members' personality system can fit into the contingency theory of organizations. This has been the major goal of this study. But we have accomplished our two secondary goals as well. First, we have expanded our understanding of the dimensions of the internal environment which must be fit to the external environment for effective performance. Where Lawrence and Lorsch identified four such dimensions, we have identified at least twice that many. However, we must reemphasize that even this expanded view is still a relatively crude map of the differences which must exist in internal environments if units are to deal effectively with external environments as varied as those represented by the manufacturing and research environments studied here. Second, we have been able to establish more strongly than did Lawrence and Lorsch that there is a clear link between unit performance and the presence of a fit between external and internal environmental forces.

With this summary view of the results of our study and their contribution to the developing contingency theory of organizations, we will return to the question of what these findings mean to the practicing administrator.

Implications for Management Practice and Research

Like other studies from the contingency perspective, the central message of our findings for managers is that there is no one best solution to the administrative and organizational issues they face. Rather, questions of managerial behavior and organizational design must be considered in light of the external environment which each organizational unit faces and the predispositions of its members. This position is at variance with the broad panaceas about management practices which have been advocated by many earlier authors. For example, it is questionable whether the earlier prescriptions of Likert and McGregor, with their emphasis on participative leadership and lower-level involvement in decisions, would lead to positive outcomes in situations like the production plants we have investigated.[2] In fact, it is interesting to note that McGregor himself, in his final book, moved to a position which was much closer to the contingency viewpoint we advocate.[3]

Similarly, the results of our study cast serious doubt on the more traditional assumptions about the individual's relationship to the organization which are held by many practicing managers. These assumptions, which have been articulated in the work of Fredrick W. Taylor, by many of the classic management theorists, and in Max Weber's theory of bureaucracy, have become a part of a prevalent management ideology in the United States.[4] They suggest that man is basically an economic creature and they emphasize the importance of financial incentives, tight control, specific job definitions, and pervasive rules as the key to an effective link between man and organization. Such an approach clearly would be unsuitable to units like the research laboratories studied here.

Stated in this way, the implications of our study and the entire contingency perspective represent a departure from much of the prior management wisdom and systematic research about man in organization. The broad implications of this new perspective for managers have been discussed by several of the contributors to it, and it is not our intention to restate their conclusions here.[5-8] Instead, we shall focus on the specific implications of our findings, showing how the characteristics of organization

[2] Rensis Likert, *The Human Organization: Its Management and Value* (New York: McGraw-Hill, 1967).

[3] Douglas McGregor, *The Professional Manager* (New York: McGraw-Hill, 1967).

[4] Frederick W. Taylor, *The Principles of Scientific Management* (New York: Harper & Row, 1911).

[5] Paul R. Lawrence and Jay W. Lorsch, *Organization and Environment* (Boston: Harvard Business School, Division of Research, 1967).

[6] Tom Burns and D. M. Stalker, *The Management of Innovation* (London: Tavistock, 1959).

[7] Joan Woodward, *Industrial Organization: Theory and Practice* (New York: Oxford University Press, 1965).

[8] Fred E. Fiedler, *A Theory of Leadership Effectiveness* (New York: McGraw-Hill, 1967).

members and the rewards they seek from work relate to the contingency approach. In so doing, we should emphasize that our view of man as having a contingent relationship to his work and organizational setting is supported by the earlier research of such organizational psychologists as Porter and Lawler, and Vroom.[9-10] Although these authors have recognized the variability in man and his organizational context, their more psychological focus does not include the wide array of internal and external environmental factors considered here. On the other hand, their work does provide a more detailed view of how the exchange relationship between man and organization seems to function. It is our hope that future work will more closely link these more psychologically oriented studies to the contingency theory of organization.

Despite the need for further research, we believe that the results of this study do provide a way of conceptualizing variables at the interface between the individual and the organization which can be utilized by practicing managers to deal with the issues they face. By examining several specific implications for the practice of management today and in the future, the balance of this chapter allows the reader to test whether our view of the utility of this model is accurate. At the same time, we shall also discuss certain additional avenues for future investigation which are suggested by these findings.

Administrative Implications

In turning to the more specific implications of this study, one is immediately confronted with a central feature of the contingency approach, one that is simultaneously its major strength and a major source of frustration in its application. This is its systemic nature. As has been emphasized, no simple causal chain can be identified; rather, the basic argument is that internal and external environmental factors and individual predispositions are intertwined. These are also interrelated in a complex fashion to individual feelings of competence and effective unit performance, factors which themselves are interdependent. How, then, does a manager decide where to intervene, if the system of variables is not producing the organizational and individual results desired? One possibility is to redefine the unit's purpose so that the external environment in which it operates is more

[9] Lyman W. Porter and Edward E. Lawler, III, *Managerial Attitudes and Performance* (Homewood, Ill.: Irwin, 1968).
[10] Victor H. Vroom, *Work and Motivation* (New York: Wiley, 1964).

consistent with internal environmental characteristics and/or individual members' predispositions. While such an approach is always possible, the probability of its being viable for a single unit imbedded in a multiunit organization seems small indeed. For example, it is unlikely that the management of any of the low-performing plants or laboratories could have redefined their missions in the context of their total organization's external environment to a sufficient extent to achieve the desired congruence among variables.

Another possibility, of course, is to achieve performance improvement by a more minor alteration of some aspect of the unit's external environment, hoping that this will result in achieving a better fit within the system of variables. Such action might include a change in prices, a modification in technology or product, etc. How this might be accomplished would vary from situation to situation, depending on market and/or technical factors.

Beyond this approach, the most promising entry point seems to be the internal environment of the unit. For example, here the manager can work on the formal organizational variables as one way of achieving better congruence between the internal and the external environmental and individual characteristics. By manipulating formal organizational variables, the manager provides a new set of signals to organization members about what is expected of them in terms of influence patterns, coordinating activity, etc. If the new set of expectations facilitates members' more effectively accomplishing their work and simultaneously fits their predispositions, they are likely to reinforce the formal pattern of expectations through their own behavior. Gradually, the characteristics of the total range of internal environmental variables should become more consistent with the external environment and members' predispositions. A closely related possibility is that of directly working on other facets of the internal environment, particularly the leadership style of managers, in a similar attempt to bring the members' behaviors and orientations more in line with external environmental requirements and individual predispositions. These two approaches seem most promising when individual characteristics and external environmental requirements are congruent with each other, but when the internal environment does not fit these factors. This was the case in all the low-performing situations we investigated. That is, the individuals in these units seemed to have chosen to work in an organization whose external environment fit their personal characteristics, but where the organizational arrangements and behavior patterns in the internal environment fit neither members' personalities nor the external environment. Since our data suggest this might be a common situation facing managers, in the next section we will explore the implications of this study for the design of organizations and for selection and development of leadership styles.

Although not encountered in this study, the possibility cannot be ignored that managers also may face a situation in which internal and external environmental features are congruent, but unmatched by individual characteristics. In such a situation, another action possibility—the attempt to alter individual predispositions through education or the infusion of new personnel—could be used. We shall investigate this possibility after attempting to discover how this study can improve our understanding of organizational design and leadership issues.

Organizational design

As a first step, it is essential to be more explicit about what is meant by *organizational design*. We use this term to refer to the planning of such formal organizational variables as the management structure, measurement and evaluation practices, reward schemes, and standardized procedures. The classic organizational theorists suggest that the two major issues with which such variables must deal are division of labor and coordination of effort.[11] This has been carried further by Lawrence and Lorsch.[12] In their application of the concepts of differentiation and integration, they concluded that the issues of division of labor and coordination were even more complex than had earlier been recognized. Division of labor resulted in differentiation among functions. In effective organizations, as the results of the current study also indicate, these differences enable each functional unit to meet the demands of its part of the external environment. However, simultaneously, these differences lead to conflicts among units which must be resolved before the integration which also accompanies effective operations can be achieved.

While Lawrence and Lorsch deal with the implications of these findings for designing organizations to achieve both the necessary differentiation and integration, the major contribution of our study to organizational design issues exists in the expanded view it provides of the concept of

---

[11] Luther Gulick and Lyndall F. Urwick, eds., *Papers on the Science of Administration* (New York: Columbia University, Institute of Public Administration, 1937).

[12] Lawrence and Lorsch, *Organization*.

differentiation. Lawrence and Lorsch discovered the importance, for organizational performance, of each functional unit's differentiated internal characteristics fitting external environmental requirements, but this study adds the human element. Further, we have identified many more formal and behavioral characteristics, along which the internal environment of functional units might need to be differentiated. For example, assume that one of the effective research laboratories and one of the effective production plants were in the same organization. We would expect to find the individuals in both gaining greater feelings of competence from their work. These units, however, would be differentiated from each other, not only in formality of organizational practices and members' goals, time, and interpersonal orientations, but also in the goal and time dimensions implicit in formal practices, the leadership style of their managers, the pattern of members' influence over decisions, and the degree of coordination within the unit. Also, the members in such units could be expected to have different predispositions, such as cognitive styles, tolerance for ambiguity, and attitudes toward authority and toward others.

In relation to designing formal organizations, the most obvious major implication of this expanded view of the concept of differentation is that managers responsible for various functional units should be encouraged to design and develop organizational practices which fit both their unit's environment and the predispositions of its members. Any pressure which top management is tempted to apply for homogeneity in organizational design across various functional units should be tested against whether it inhibits any of the units from developing a fit among its internal environment, the external environment, and its members.

In evaluating the design of a particular unit's formal organization, a central issue is the amount of control over members' individual work activity which would be imposed in the internal environment. This study, as well as previous contingency studies, suggests that the amount of control which is appropriate is related to the certainty of the unit's environment.[13-14] But our data also suggest that the appropriate degree of control designed into an organization must be consistent with members' attitudes toward authority. Where members prefer more dependent authority relationships, more control from the formal organization would seem appropriate. In units where members prefer more autonomy, less emphasis

[13] Lawrence and Lorsch, *Organization.*
[14] Burns and Stalker, *The Management.*

on formal controls seems desirable. Similarly, members' tolerance for ambiguity and the integrative complexity of their thought processes must fit the degree of control over their individual activity which is designed into formal organization. For those units whose members have low tolerance for ambiguity and/or low integrative complexity, greater organizational control seems to be appropriate. Less organizational control is suitable for those members who have a higher tolerance for ambiguity and greater integrative complexity. The relationship between these individual and environmental variables and organizational control over individual activity is summarized schematically in Fig. 6-2.

The elements in an organization's formal design which can be used to achieve control over individual activity are many. For example, the number of supervisors in the unit in relation to its total members (the *span of supervisory control,* according to classical terminology) can be varied to facilitate supervisors exercising close or loose control over subordinates.

Fig. 6-2. Organizational control as a contingent variable.

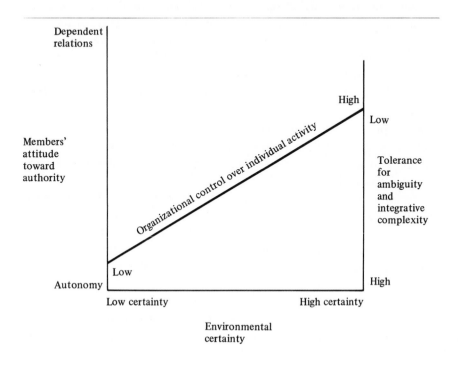

Operating procedures and/or rules are another vehicle which can be used to control behavior. Where detailed rules or procedures are prescribed about activities, members' autonomy is likely to be more limited. Similarly, the extent to which measurement and compensation practices are tied to specific detailed results is another way in which the organizational design can be manipulated to affect the degree of control over members. The exact configuration of these organizational design variables which makes sense, given the uncertainty of a particular unit's external environment and its members' predispositions, is something each manager must fit to the specifics of his situation. However, our findings suggest that the total pattern must be designed so that the organizational variables provide a consistent set of signals to members about how much autonomy they are allowed. When these signals create an internal environment which fits the external realities facing the unit and the individuals' predispositions about autonomy and ambiguity, the results should be both effective unit performance and greater feelings of competence for the individual.

Selecting the appropriate design of these organizational variables will undoubtedly be easier when, as was the case in the sites we studied, the environmental and individual variables summarized in Fig. 6-2 are all positioned at the same end of their continua. When this is not the case, the design problem becomes more difficult and the manager will have to use his own judgment to develop the most appropriate configuration of formal variables. Nonetheless, at least we have identified more precisely the individual and environmental variables which must be considered in such a judgment.

So far our focus has been on the extent to which organizational design variables can be used to control the behavior of members in their individual activities. However, a second design issue, related to organizational control within a unit, is the extent to which members must coordinate their efforts within the unit. The data shown in Fig. 6-3 suggest that the extent to which organizational control toward coordinated effort is appropriate is related to two factors. First, it seems to be contingent upon the extent to which coordination is required by the external environment. Where tighter coordination is a necessity, the organizational design can be used to achieve this end. If less coordination among members is necessary, then the need for formal organizational control to achieve coordination also seems less necessary (as the data from the research laboratories suggest). Second, the appropriate amount of organizational control to achieve coor-

Fig. 6-3. Organizational control of coordinated effort as a contingent variable.

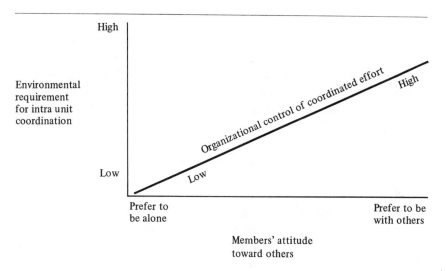

dination may also be contingent on members' attitudes toward others. Where members prefer close relationships with others, more control devoted to achieving coordination may be appropriate; where members prefer less contact with others, control which encourages coordination may be less appropriate.

The extent to which members' attitudes toward others will form a constraint on achieving coordinated effort probably will depend on the organizational design elements which are used to achieve coordination. Where design elements such as a schedule, plan, or measurement scheme are used to influence members' behavior toward a coordinated end, little contact with others may be required. Even persons who prefer to work alone may find such a system compatible. Where the means of coordination in the organization require more face-to-face contact—for example, meetings, teams, committees, etc.—the individual's attitude toward working with others can have a definite bearing on whether he would find such an organization a satisfying place to work.

Before turning to one other implication of this study for organizational design decisions, we should stress again that our findings offer no simple prescriptions for designing formal controls into organizations. But they do suggest a series of individual and external environmental dimensions that seem to have a contingent relationship to the degree of formal control which is appropriate for unit performance and individual feelings of competence. It is our hope that managers struggling with problems of designing formal organization for their units will find these relationships helpful guidelines for their thinking. In deliberating about the issue of organizational control, we are not suggesting it is possible to ignore such traditional criteria as the economic costs of supervision, the capabilities of individuals, the geographic dispersion of subordinates, etc. Rather, we are suggesting that the factors we have identified need to be considered along with these criteria. Finally, we are not suggesting that in units with low formal organizational control there is a total absence of any control over members' behavior. Rather, we are suggesting that instead of such control existing in the formal organizational arrangements, it should exist in the social controls imposed by the norms of the organization or of the members' profession, and/or within the individuals themselves as they use their personal values as a guide to appropriate behavior. As we suggested in Chapter 4, these forms of control appeared to be especially strong among the scientists in the laboratory sites.

One final distinctive ramification of this study for organizational design, which is worthy of mention, is the notion that formal practices can also vary in the time and goal dimensions emphasized. In designing measurement, evaluation, and reward schemes, this means that attention must be paid, not only to how much control, but also to the selection of criteria which are consistent with the goal orientations members must have. Similarly, these schemes must be planned to provide feedback about individual and unit performance at intervals which are consistent with the time horizons necessary to cope effectively with the external environment.

Here, as well as earlier in this discussion, we assume that the design of these formal variables is important because they will play a part in shaping the internal environment of the unit. Emphasizing particular time and goal dimensions in formal practices can lead to members' focusing on these goals and time-spans, just as designing organizational elements with a particular degree of control will have an impact on the pattern of coordination, influence, and supervisory behavior which develops in the unit. Yet, we should reemphasize that while this set of variables is accessible to managers as an important method of giving signals to subordinates about their expected behavior, our data suggest that it will only be effective in motivating individuals to outstanding performance if it is consistent with both their personalities and the external environmental requirements they face. Like the other variables in our model, these formal characteristics are truly interdependent with the other elements.

This statement allows us to highlight the major contribution of this study to a manager's thinking about organizational design. Much of the earlier rationale for making contingency prescriptions about organization design has been that a congruence between organizational characteristics and external environment will somehow lead to effective unit performance. However there has been little attention to how the individual fits into this context. Now, with the individual as part of the equation, we have learned that congruence must be achieved, not only between the unit's internal environment and its external environment, but also between these variables and the individual's predispositions. By designing organizations to fit external requirements and individual characteristics, we are not only providing individuals with a pattern of information about environmental conditions which leads to effective decision-making and implementation, but one which also provides feedback, thus enabling the individual to feel more competent. This means that not only is the design of formal organizational practices important, but also of importance is the way in which these practices are used by superiors to enhance their subordinates' feelings of competence. Again, from our data, it would appear that there is no one best way for managers to use these practices, but, if we turn to the implications of this study for managerial leadership, we can understand how the contingent relationships we have identified can contribute to our understanding of this process.

Managerial leadership

While the formal organizational design variables are one set of mechanisms for affecting the internal environment in which organization members act, another way to shape many of the behavioral variables with which we have been concerned is through the behavior of persons in leadership positions. In essence, our concern now is with how effectively managers lead the subordinate members of their units.

In this discussion, it is important to clearly define *leadership behavior*. This is necessary because of the large amount of work psychologists and sociologists have done in studying leadership. In leadership studies, as in other facets of the behavioral sciences, one result of a proliferation of studies seems to be a proliferation in the definition of the phenomena under investigation. For example, Fiedler lists ten different definitions of leadership behavior from the literature ranging from Dubin's, "Leadership is the exercise of authority and making of decisions," to Homans', "The leader is the man who comes closest to realizing the norms the group values highest; this conformity gives him his high rank, which attracts people and implies the right to assume control of the group." [15]

Without laboring over the merits of all the possible definitions, we shall use Fiedler's own definition which states that leadership behavior is: "the particular acts in which a leader engages in the course of directing and coordinating the work of his group members. This may involve such acts as structuring the work relations, praising or criticizing group members, and showing consideration for their welfare and feelings." [16] From our perspective, the advantage of this definition is that it focuses on the activities and interactions a leader carries out. This also provides a way of dealing with the issues raised implicitly by definitions such as Dubin's and Homans' about the source of the leader's power. Our data suggest that such power would seem to stem, not only from one's formal position, but also from the leader's skill in carrying out his leadership activities so that subordinates can work effectively and gain feelings of competence.

The aspects of leadership behavior on which we shall focus are two: the leader's efforts to direct and coordinate work activities, including the resolution of conflict; and his methods of providing feedback to subordinates about their own and the unit's performance. Before turning to these topics, however, we need to describe briefly the general state of the leadership literature.

As in the case of organizational design, much of the work on leadership has attempted to find a universal approach to effectiveness. Fiedler points to two opposing views which have developed in this quest. One which is prevalent in traditional supervisory and management training in industry, government, and especially in the military, holds that the leader "must be decisive, . . . must think and plan for the group, and that the responsibility for directing, controlling, coordinating, and evaluating the group members' actions is primarily his and cannot be shifted to others." [17] The reader will recognize that this view is closely akin to the classical organizational theorists' assumption about organizational design. This is not

---

[15] Fiedler, *A Theory,* pp. 7-8.
[16] Fiedler, *A Theory,* p. 36.
[17] Fiedler, *A Theory,* p. 13.

merely a coincidence, but results from the fact that this leadership view has emerged from Taylor's *Principles of Scientific Management,* and has been expanded by many of the classicists cited above.[18-20] The second viewpoint, which Fiedler attributes to the human relations theorists such as McGregor and Likert, maintains the leader will be most effective when he can call out the creativity and the willing cooperation of his men and that he can do this most effectively only when he can get his group members to participate in the decision-making processes and the direction of group action." [21]

Fiedler himself spells out a contingency model of leadership effectiveness which delineates the specific conditions under which various leadership styles are most appropriate. The factors which he has examined are: leader-member relations; the power position of the leader; and the task structure. In essence, he has found that leaders whose personalities orient them to task concerns are more effective when the configuration of these factors make the leader's job either very difficult or very easy. When these three conditions are only moderately favorable, the most effective leader will be one whose personality is more oriented to maintaining interpersonal relationships within his group of subordinates. However, there is one important difference between Fiedler's work and our own approach to these issues. Fiedler has not considered differences among individuals in their predispositions toward authority, as we have done.

Tannenbaum and Schmidt, although they use different variables to describe leadership behavior and situational variables, also have noted what amounts to a contingency approach to leadership issues.[22] They see leadership behaviors as falling along a continuum from "boss centered" to "subordinate centered." According to their view, effective leadership behavior will depend upon the manager's own personality, the personalities of his subordinates, and the organizational and task situations he faces.

While our own study has not focused on leadership to the depth that Fielder or Tannenbaum and Schmidt have, and while we have not used identical variables, our general conclusion is consistent with theirs. What constitutes effective leadership behavior for managers depends upon the

[18] Taylor, *The Principles.*
[19] Gulick, *Papers.*
[20] Henri Fayol, *Industrial and General Administration* (Paris: Dunod, 1925).
[21] Fiedler, *A Theory*, p. 13.
[22] Robert Tannenbaum and Warren H. Schmidt, "How to Choose a Leadership Pattern," *Harvard Business Review* 36 (March-April 1958):95-101.

nature of the external environment in which their unit is operating, as well as on the other variables present in the internal environment and the personality attributes of their subordinates. In the effective research laboratories, managers directed and coordinated efforts by apparently encouraging participation in decision-making, which, as we have seen, was consistent with external requirements and professionals who preferred autonomy. The plant managers in the effective sites appeared to rely on a more directive approach in supervision and coordination of their subordinates' efforts. This, too, was consistent with the external requirements facing these units and the predispositions of plant personnel, who were not uncomfortable with stronger authority relationships. It should be emphasized that these plant managers were not completely autocratic; as the data in Chapter 4 indicates, they also seemed to encourage participation a fair amount of the time. Rather, the point is that the managers in the high-performing manufacturing sites were more directive than were their counterparts in the less effective plants and also more directive than were the research administrators in the effective laboratories.

Thus, our findings, as well as those of Fiedler and Tannenbaum and Schmidt, suggest that managers who are concerned with developing more effective leadership patterns must analyze the situational variables involved to determine what behavior will most likely be effective. If the reader were to compare these three works, he might conclude that such advice was fine in theory, but difficult to put into practice because of the range of variables these authors consider. Yet, a more careful look at their findings suggests several major factors which they have jointly identified as being important in determining what leadership style will be effective in a given situation. For example, our own findings and those of Fiedler and of Tannenbaum and Schmidt indicate that the dimension of the actual work which is crucial is determined by how well understood, structured, or certain it is. Similarly, this study and Fiedler's work suggest that a second important factor is the extent to which the organization supports its leaders with positional power to control subordinates. Further, Tannenbaum and Schmidt's findings and our own suggest that another crucial organizational factor is the extent to which subordinates are accustomed to involvement in decisions. Finally, our work and that of Tannenbaum and Schmidt converge on three characteristics of subordinates' personalities which relate to effective leadership behavior; that is, predispositions for independence, tolerance for ambiguity, and the knowledge and information which subordinates have to contribute to decisions.

TABLE 6-2 A Contingency Approach to Leadership

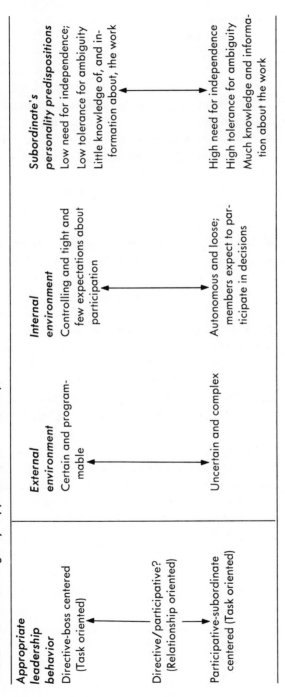

Appropriate leadership behavior	External environment	Internal environment	Subordinate's personality predispositions
Directive-boss centered (Task oriented)	Certain and programmable	Controlling and tight and few expectations about participation	Low need for independence; Low tolerance for ambiguity Little knowledge of, and information about, the work
Directive/participative? (Relationship oriented)			
Participative-subordinate centered (Task oriented)	Uncertain and complex	Autonomous and loose; members expect to participate in decisions	High need for independence High tolerance for ambiguity Much knowledge and information about the work

Table 6-2 summarizes the contingencies which seem to be overlapping in our work and in Fielder's and Tannenbaum and Schmidt's. It also indicates the leadership behavior appropriate to the situations contained in the table. In the situation noted at the top of the table, this study suggests that a more directive approach would be effective, which is identical with Tannenbaum and Schmidt's conclusion about the appropriateness of a boss-centered style under these same conditions. Similarly, in the situation noted at the bottom of Table 6-2, our conclusions and those of Tannenbaum and Schmidt would urge more participative or subordinate-centered behavior in directing and controlling activities.

By focusing only on a directive vs. participative continuum, this formulation has not yet considered the task vs. the relationship dimension of leadership behavior identified by Fiedler. Since, in view of the complexity of man's behavior, it seems reasonable to assume that the richness of a leader's interactions cannot be described along just one dimension, we can add Fiedler's dimension also. To do so, we must recognize that Fiedler defines the *favorableness* of a situation to a leader as "the degree to which the situation enables the leader to exert influence over the group." [23] Some may argue with the definition, but if it is accepted we can generally conclude that the characteristics listed at the top of Table 6-2 represent a situation which, in Fiedler's terms, is favorable to the leader, while those at the bottom present the leader with more unfavorable and difficult situations. Combining our findings with Fiedler's, it seems that a directive, *task-oriented* style of leadership is appropriate under the conditions at the top of Table 6-2 (which Fiedler labels "favorable"), while under those at the bottom (which Fiedler calls "unfavorable"), a participative, *task-oriented* style is necessary. In the middle range of conditions (which Fiedler would call "moderately favorable"), it is still an open question as to whether a leader would be more effective combining Fiedler's recommended *relationship-oriented* leadership style with more directive or participative behavior. This would require further investigation since our own work and that of Tannenbaum and Schmidt have dealt only with the extreme conditions.

In proposing this model of leadership effectiveness, we do not imply that the variables identified by these other authors which have not been included are not important [e.g., leader's relation with group (Fielder); orga-

---

[23] Fiedler, *A Theory,* p. 13.

nizational size, subordinate's interest in problem and identification with organizational goals (Tannenbaum and Schmidt)]. Rather, we suggest that there is not yet enough agreement about them to consider them as useful as the other variables identified for thinking about leadership issues.

Assuming that the reader accepts this synthesis as a useful way of classifying the appropriate leadership behavior for directing and coordinating subordinates under different conditions, the question of how can it be used remains. Certainly, a major problem in its application is noted by Fiedler and by Tannenbaum and Schmidt. This is the fact that a leader's actual style is closely tied to his personality and is difficult to alter. Our assumptions about individual personality outlined in earlier chapters are also consistent with this view. A person's behavior pattern is shaped not only by the current stimuli he meets, but also by a consistent history of personality development and by his biological makeup.

This point makes it difficult to argue for leadership training (whether it be the conventional sort or a laboratory approach) as a panacea to change a pattern of leadership behavior which is highly inconsistent with the situation. Certainly, however, such training can be useful in helping managers gain greater awareness of their own styles, and in helping them to adapt their behavior (albeit within a narrow range) to the demands of the situation. Even when such training is useful, it should be emphasized that it must be tailored to the requirements of the particular situation. Although the goal of much leadership training over the past decade has been to encourage more participative leadership, it is entirely possible that in settings such as the production plants in this study, the emphasis should be equally placed on creating more effective directive leadership. This means that the training experts and the managers involved in planning such training need to make a careful analysis of the situational conditions which influence the participants of a training program and must plan the program to help the participants develop a leadership pattern consistent with the particular conditions they face on their jobs and with their own personalities.

An even more useful application of this model to leadership issues is personnel selection and placement. The contingency approach can be very useful to managers as they select candidates for managerial positions and as they think about moving subordinates from one unit to another. It can provide guidelines for thinking more clearly about which managers will be most effective in particular positions. We shall return to this point in dealing with the broader issues of personnel selection, but first we will consider another application of our findings to leadership behavior.

Regardless of environmental or individual characteristics, we found in effective units a greater tendency to confront conflict than was present in the less effective units. Recognizing that one of the important functions of a superior in any unit is the resolution of conflicts among subordinates, it follows that an important behavioral dimension of leaders in effective units is to bring conflicts into the open and work them through. While there is uniformity in the pattern of leadership in both sets of effective units, the differences in their approaches to directing and coordinating activities suggest that the manner in which conflict is confronted will also vary. In units such as the effective plants, we can surmise that leaders may have involved subordinates in working through conflicts, but that they were also willing to take the initiative and be more directive in searching for solutions. Apparently, they were able to accomplish this without their subordinates feeling that these solutions were forced on them. Perhaps this resulted because the superior was able to assemble the necessary information to develop an effective solution and his subordinates recognized this fact. In the laboratories, the leaders apparently were more completely involved with subordinates in the confrontation of conflict, which was necessitated, no doubt, because the subordinates themselves had more of the knowledge relevant to resolving the problems.

Further research is needed to test whether our speculations about these differences are valid. If they are found to be so, this has implications for training managers to use a more confronting approach in dealing with conflict. Such training efforts have been described by Blake and Mouton and Beckhard among others, and seem generally to be effective.[24-25] However, one major drawback is that they do not explicitly recognize the differences in leadership patterns which we have been discussing. Hopefully, future efforts in this direction will take seriously the contingent approach we have outlined and tailor such training efforts to help managers incorporate the confrontation of conflict into the style of leadership which is appropriate for them and their situation. While management education and training can improve leadership effectiveness as suggested above, a

[24] Robert Blake and Jane Mouton, *The Managerial Grid* (Houston: Gulf, 1964).
[25] Richard Beckhard, *Organization Development: Strategies and Models* (Reading, Mass.: Addison-Wesley, 1969).

better long-term solution is to select managers whose personalities suit the particular subordinates and the environmental conditions present.

Personnel Selection

For many managers, mentioning personnel selection raises the specter of such issues as personality tests and their validity, or the issue of how much influence personnel specialists and/or line managers should have on selection decisions. It is our intention to avoid these traditional issues; instead, we will examine the implications of this study for personnel selection in a broader prospect.

At the outset, we must recognize that the decision to join a particular organization in a specific position is a mutual decision, involving both the individual and a representative of higher management of the organization. Thus, the problem with which we are concerned is one of career or job choice for the individual on the one hand, and of personnel selection and placement for the organization on the other. While, in any particular instance, these two decisions interact with the result that man and organization engage each other, it is useful to discuss the implications from each side of the equation separately.

As the previous discussion of leadership has suggested, a major implication of this study is that it provides a way of thinking about matching an individual having a particular personality and leadership style to an organizational-environmental setting. While our previous focus was on leaders and the leadership position, the model which we have developed appears to be equally useful in thinking about the selection of personnel for those professional and managerial positions which do not greatly involve the direction and coordination of others.

In practice, most approaches to personnel selection have usually emphasized the identification of those personality characteristics which may lead to effective performance, but have devoted less attention to understanding the internal and external environmental variables which exist in a particular situation. The advantage of the conceptual approach which this study has produced is that it provides a way of linking individual characteristics to the other variables in the work setting so that both the individual and the organization can achieve important benefits.

Of course, at the present stage of its development, our model provides only a broad approach to the problems of personnel selection and placement. More work is required to identify a wider range of personality variables and, perhaps more importantly, to understand the fit between man, job, and organization in a wider range of job settings. Particularly important, as mentioned earlier, is obtaining greater understanding of how these variables interact in situations where the external environment is not as highly certain as those facing the plants or as highly uncertain as those facing the laboratories in this study.

As we have also suggested, the view of human personality put forth here makes the issues of improving personnel selection crucial. If, as the work of Erikson and others who have studied personality development suggests, man's capacity for growth and change are constrained by his prior personal history and biological makeup, then the prospects for achieving a better fit between man and organization through training and education will always be limited.[26] In those situations where the characteristics of individuals do not fit environmental and organizational conditions, placement and selection are important factors in achieving an improved balance between man and organization.

From the perspective of the individual seeking a position, this view of personality makes his choice of job and career crucial. The contingency approach can be useful for such an individual, whether he is a young college or professional school graduate or a more experienced professional manager. This is well demonstrated by the plight of the personnel in the low-performing sites. In their personality dimensions they were identical to those of their counterparts in the effective units, but they had joined an organizational unit whose internal environment matched neither their personalities nor the units' external environment. As a result, they did not achieve strong feelings of competence from their work. While we have little or no evidence on how these individuals came to join these organizations, it is reasonable to speculate that it was a result of career choices which pointed them to careers as manufacturing managers and engineers or industrial researchers. Their choices probably were made at the completion of their formal education or shortly thereafter. They were also most likely based on complex factors in their earlier personal history about which they may have been largely unaware.[27] The managers joined their units over a long period of time, and many may have actually joined at a time when

---

[26] Erik H. Erikson, "Identity and the Life Cycle," in *Childhood and Society* (New York: Norton, 1963).

[27] Gene Dalton, Louis Barnes, and Abraham Zaleznik, *Orientation and Conflict in Careers* (Boston: Harvard Business School, Division of Research, 1970).

there was a reasonable fit among their personalities and the units' internal and external environmental attributes. Nonetheless, the fact remains that this contingency approach could have been useful in determining the suitability of a new position or in evaluating why they found their current position so unsatisfying.

Too often prospective employees look at a new position in terms of such factors as income, location, or the intrinsic nature of the work without really considering whether the total organizational situation and the work will provide a good fit for their personalities. It would appear far wiser for individuals to develop some awareness of both their own proclivities and the organizational situation before making a job choice. Sample questions that individuals might ask are: Do I like working in a setting where strong leadership is present or where I will have more autonomy? Do I prefer to work closely with peers or alone? How much ambiguity can I tolerate? Does the organization in question match my tendencies and does it fit the nature of the work to be done? While the individual job-seeker needs to ask such questions, it is equally important that the employer provides accurate information to enable individuals to assess the suitability of a particular job setting to themselves. How much control does the organization impose on its members? How much ambiguity is present? Do members usually work alone or together? If the individual seeking a position makes a careful self-assessment and gets the answers to questions such as these, it will be helpful both for him and his potential employer. It will assure both that there is the greater likelihood of the individual making the most of his potential and contributing to the success of the organization.

Providing performance feedback

Viewing the selection process in this manner also provides a new way of thinking about giving feedback to organization members. One implication of our findings is that any feedback to the individual about his or her performance has an important psychological impact. Such feedback is an important basis upon which the individual judges his competence. The person who gets positive data about his performance will feel rewarded because of his enhanced sense of competence and, in the future, will continue to strive to achieve greater feelings of competence. However, for the individual who is not performing up to his superior's expectations, the problem is more complex, and it is here we shall focus our discussion.

Traditionally, the person who does not live up to management's expectation about performance is viewed as a failure. If his performance does not improve, he is liable to be dismissed. The result of this traditional approach is a strong, often permanently damaging, lowered sense of competence for the individual. Since the blame is placed on the "poor performer," no effort is made by the organization to assess whether he really was a good *fit* for the job, and/or whether there was a reasonable fit between the organizational arrangement and the work to be done. Using the contingency model, however, a manager would be more likely to view poor performance by an individual as linked to a lack of fit. If investigation revealed that the lack of suitability was present between the organizational arrangement and the work itself, attempts could be made to bring the elements into congruence. If, however, the lack of fit was between the person on the one hand and the external and internal environments on the other, his removal from the organization might still be necessary. Even in this event, the manager making this decision should find the contingency model helpful in counseling the low-performing subordinate about the causes of his difficulty and in helping him to think through other options. Most important, if such a situation were well handled, the subordinate could leave not with a sense of being punished for failure, but, rather, with a clearer understanding of his strengths and limitations, and of what settings could more adequately match his strengths.

It would be naïve to suggest that this application will be easily adopted by managers for at least two reasons. First, there seems to be a pervasive and deep-rooted feeling in the United States that poor performance is a matter of personal failure. Second, on this issue, as well as on many others, managers prefer simple solutions. In dealing with the low performer, as in the other applications we have discussed, the contingency approach does not offer a simplistic cure. Rather, it encourages managers to face the real complexity of the human issues they face. While this may be a more difficult course, the evidence of this and of the earlier contingency studies suggests it will lead to better results for both the individual and the organization. This is so, not only in dealing with a problem subordinate, but for the broader issues of organization design, leadership, and selection that we have been discussing.

Broader Implications for Understanding Man and Organization

So far our discussion has centered on the implications of this study for professional and managerial employees and the organizations in which they labor. However, the general contingency approach may have broader implications for other problems in our industrial society. For example, a crucial issue facing many industrial firms is the motivation and productivity of industrial workers. Evidence of discontent and frustration among all these so-called blue-collar workers is widespread in the popular and business press.[28] Projections for the future suggest these problems are not likely to abate and, in fact, they may become even more intense among white-collar employees.[29] Further evidence that this is a crucial problem is provided by the economic difficulties facing the United States in the world market. While monetary and economic policy may provide remedies, a central issue seems to be the relative productivity of the U.S. work force vs. European and Japanese workers. While part of this hiatus may be overcome through technological improvements, it appears that technology alone is not the answer. What is also required is a better approach to managing the interface between workers, organization, and technology.

The model developed here suggests a broad approach to attacking the problem. While our study has been directed toward managerial and professional personnel, two other studies of industrial workers suggest that the hypothesis that a fit between man, technology, and organization can lead to greater productivity and individual well-being may be a fruitful one to pursue. First, Turner and Lawrence reported that workers from larger cities tended to be more satisfied with relatively simple and uncomplicated jobs.[30] In contrast, workers from smaller towns tended to be much more satisfied with more complex tasks. The authors concluded that the town workers, as compared to the city workers, wanted a relatively large amount of variety, autonomy, interaction, and responsibility in their jobs. Each group was most satisfied working with a technology and within an organization which fit predispositions they had developed as they grew up in their particular communities. Blauner makes a parallel point.[31] He also found that workers had varying attitudes toward their work, depending on whether there was a fit between their predispositions and the work situation, including the technology. For example, in the automobile industry, which involves

---

[28] See, for example, Judson Gooding, "Blue-Collar Blues on the Assembly Line," *Fortune* (July 1970):68-71.

[29] Wickham Skinner, "The Anachronistic Factory," *Harvard Business Review* 49 (January-February, 1971):61-70.

[30] Arthur N. Turner and Paul R. Lawrence, *Industrial Jobs and the Worker* (Boston: Harvard Business School, Division of Research, 1965).

[31] Robert Blauner, *Alienation and Freedom* (Chicago: University of Chicago Press, 1964).

a highly certain task, workers were alienated from the company and its goals by an inability to influence the work situation, a loss of meaning in the work, a sense of being isolated, and a lack of any involvement in the task. Textile workers, who had tasks similar to the automobile workers, were not so alienated. One reason was that through a socialization process in family and community the textile workers were taught not to expect meaning in their work, whereas the automobile workers apparently expected more from their jobs.

While these two studies and our own findings suggest that a contingency strategy for understanding the relationship between industrial workers and their work would be fruitful, more investigation is needed. The studies of Turner and Lawrence and Blauner, although generally consistent, are contradictory in specific detail. The variables each used are different from each other's and from ours. Most important in this regard, neither of the earlier studies has treated feelings of competence as a reward for the work itself. Further, reports of innovations in organization and job design in several factories suggest that job enrichment and more involvement in decision-making for workers can lead both to greater productivity and higher morale.[32] Whether these experiments provide general support for a universal new approach to managing the work force based on more worker participation and more complex jobs, or whether they are simply a case of achieving a good fit among workers' needs, technology, and organization, is an open question requiring more investigation. It is interesting to note, however, that many of these approaches have been carried out in plants which are small, with relatively uncertain technologies (e.g., electronics, instruments, food processing), and with workers from a rural setting.[33] This suggests to us that these cases may involve either intentionally or unintentionally achieving a good fit between the variables in the contingency model. This fit then supports workers in achieving effective performance and high feelings of competence.

The view that feelings of competence may be important sources of motivation for any individual (including blue-collar and clerical employees) in a work setting, precisely because they are derived from the performance of the

[32] Judson Gooding, "It Pays to Wake Up the Blue-Collar Worker," *Fortune* (September 1970):132-5.

[33] Richard E. Walton, "How to Counter Alienation in the Plant," *Harvard Business Review* 50 (November-December, 1972):70.

job itself, finds support from the work of Herzberg.[34] It appears that an individual's sense of competence can come from the successful mastering of *any* work environment, either routine or rapidly changing and ambiguous, that fits his or her predispositions. Moreover, there seems to be no diminishing of the motivation to perform effectively once one level of feelings of competence has been attained. Rather, the achievement of a sense of competence from successfully doing one job seems to spur the individual on to behave effectively so as to maintain and increase this intrinsic reward. These kinds of expectations may even become more important to the individual as they become better satisfied.[35]

In the same vein, Locke suggests that any individual will aim for high performance on the job provided he believes that the high performance is possible and to the extent that he believes it will lead to attaining job values which are important personally.[36] Our study suggests a way of supporting this view in terms of the motivation and productivity of industrial blue-collar and clerical workers. We would hypothesize, first, that individuals at any level in the organization are more likely to believe high performance is possible if internal environmental characteristics and their own personality preferences fit the external environmental requirements and, second, that individuals at any level in the organization might define a sense of competence at work as an important job-related reward.

While these are the conclusions to which our work and others' studies lead us, we do not ask the reader to accept this interpretation and its implication for dealing with the critical questions of work-force productivity. Rather, we would argue for an open mind on the applicability of the contingency approach to these issues while more research is conducted to answer a number of basic questions such as: Is sense of competence as important a source of motivation for industrial and clerical workers as it appears to be for managerial and professional employees? Are there differences in the importance of sense of competence at work among various subcultures in the United States and among cultures overseas? Are the predispositions of younger workers significantly different from those of older

[34] Frederick Herzberg, "One More Time: How Do You Motivate Employees?" *Harvard Business Review* 46 (January-February 1968):53-62; and Frederick Herzberg, et al., *The Motivation to Work* (New York: Wiley, 1959).

[35] C. P. Alderfer, "An Empirical Test of a New Theory of Human Needs," *Organizational Behavior and Human Performance* 4 (1969):142-175.

[36] Edwin A. Locke, "Job Satisfaction and Job Performance: A Theoretical Analysis," *Organizational Behavior and Human Performance* 5 (1970): 484-500.

workers? What are the relevant technological and organizational variables which must be matched to worker predispositions?

A straightforward method of initially addressing such questions and determining whether our approach has validity for this class of problems would be to launch a comparative study of several industrial plants to learn if there is a connection between the level of worker discontent and the fit among technological, organizational, and personality variables. Such a study would provide insights into the important current difficulties in motivating industrial and service workers and also further our understanding of man in organization. Increasing our knowledge about the relationship between the individual and the organization is crucial for the immediate future and for the longer term as well. Even a cursory glance at the proliferating literature about what the future may hold suggests that achieving a balanced relationship between the individual and the organization for all types of employees will be increasingly complicated.[37] A younger, more socially oriented work force; more women and minority group members in higher managerial posts; more temporary organizations that come together to solve problems, disbanding when a solution is reached; a shorter work week; and more formal education for more people are just a few of the predictions of what the future may bring to organizational life.

These predictions, like many speculations about the future, may be overstated. Clearly, however, there is no evidence that more certain work, such as that in the manufacturing plants in this study, will disappear. Nor do we find any clear evidence that relatively dependent persons who dislike ambiguity and uncertainty will suddenly disappear from the earth. Yet, we cannot ignore the evidence which suggests a gradual shift in the nature and values of work forces and organizations. This view suggests that managers and social scientists alike will have to maintain an awareness of how the external and internal environmental and individual variables considered in this study are shifting. They will then have to maintain a fit among them, even as they change.

Some readers undoubtedly will feel that such a conclusion is too conservative in that it does not recognize what they consider to be the sweep toward more humanistic values in all facets of our society, including work organizations. Their argument would be that managers must increasingly care about the self-worth of the individuals who work for and with them

---

[37] See, for example, Alvin Toffler, *Future Shock* (New York: Random House, 1970).

and must increasingly tap the full potential of the human resources available to them. Our response to this position is that too often this caring for the individual and the goals of human resource utilization are based on notions that all persons are pretty much alike in the needs that brought them into the work organization. On that ground, we believe that such a humanistic view is inadequate. For us, a real humanism must acknowledge, appreciate, and account for differences in people. We make no normative judgments about people and their differences. We accept them and attempt to account for them. The persons studied here were found to be very dissimilar. Some liked structured organization, more directive supervision, and certainty in their work; others preferred opposite conditions. However, in one way all these individuals seemed alike; they all sought to feel competent from mastering their work. The behavior through which some attained this sense of competence may not have made sense to others.

The humanism for which we opt, however, makes no such judgment. Rather, it encourages the individual to seek his sense of competence in the manner he himself defines from his own personality; and it encourages the organization to provide the individual with the opportunity to attain his sense of competence from his work. In linking a sense of competence at work with differing personality patterns, we are highlighting the dignity and worth of every man in the organization. We are taking an approach that stresses what each man really is—himself—and not what we normatively want all men to be like.

There are also those who will argue that this approach does not account for the human potential for growth and change. For example, Argyris has argued that man has the capacity to grow into a more self-governing and open creature, but is constrained from doing so by the character of many of our existing organizational arrangements.[38] Our argument with this position is twofold. First, the issue is not whether man has a potential for growth; rather, the point is that the direction of growth is less constrained by the present-day institutions in which a person works than it is by his genetic makeup and by his socialization in early childhood and adolescent development. As noted earlier, there is plentiful evidence of this fact in the work of scholars such as Erikson who are concerned with human development.[39] Man's growth and development takes place in small incre-

[38] Chris Argyris, *Integrating the Individual and the Organization* (New York: Wiley, 1964).
[39] Erikson, "Identity."

ments and always in a direction which is consistent with his past development. The second argument we have with a posture such as Argyris's, has to do with its inherent normative nature. Basically, the thrust of this argument seems to be that all men should grow to be less dependent and more autonomous and open. It is our belief that no one direction of growth will make sense for all men. Achieving a fit between the individual's character, his job, and the organization in which he spends his working life will enable him to grow by developing his feelings of competence in his own unique way. This seems to be the most practical way to enable the individual to achieve the growth he seeks and defines for himself.

Finally, our view of the individual in the organization also can eliminate the dichotomy between organizational effectiveness and the individual's personal fulfillment. If the findings of this study stand the test of time and criticism, we may no longer need to be as concerned with the traditional discussion about the trade-off between organizational performance and rewards for the individual. An important fulfillment for the individual can come from a job mastered successfully. This, in turn, means the organization will be more likely to achieve its goals. Rather than suggesting a dichotomy between organizational effectiveness and individual fulfillment, the contingency approach suggests that there can be a true integration of individual and organizational growth and development.

Methodological
appendix

The description of the research techniques used in this study will be organized around the major variables measured: characteristics of the external environment; characteristics of unit members; and dimensions of the internal environment. More detailed information about the developmental stages of the methodology appears in Morse's "Internal Organizational Patterning and Sense of Competence Motivation," and in Lawrence and Lorsch's *Organization and Environment*.[1-2]

The External Environment

The external environment questionnaire

The following questionnaire, administered to top officials in the companies from which each pair of sites was selected and to the top two or three people in each laboratory or production plant, was designed to mea-

[1] John J. Morse, "Internal Organizational Patterning and Sense of Competence Motivation (Ph.D. diss., Harvard University Graduate School of Business Administration, 1969).

[2] Paul R. Lawrence and Jay W. Lorsch, *Organization and Environment* (Boston: Harvard Business School, Division of Research, 1967).

sure their perceptions of the characteristics of the external environment. These data were used to validate our a priori assumptions about the nature of such external environments. The first question measured the clarity of information in the external environment, the second measured the time-span for performance feedback, and the third its programmability. Scores for the three dimensions were added and averaged.[3]

---

[3] The reason for combining scores rests on their conceptual interrelationship. See Lawrence and Lorsch, *Organization,* p. 28*n.*

Due to rapid change in a unit, or the state of development in the technology used in the unit, etc., unit executives often have varying degrees of certainty concerning what their unit job requirements are and the kinds of activities their units *must* engage in to achieve these requirements. The following series of questions is an effort to obtain data concerning this aspect of certainty in your unit.

A. Please circle the point on the scale provided which most nearly describes the degree to which present job requirements in your department or unit are clearly stated or known:

Job requirements are very clear in most instances   1   2   3   4   5   6   7   Job requirements are not at all clear in most instances

B. Please check the alternative which most nearly describes the typical length of time involved before feedback is available to your unit concerning the success of its job performance:

_____ (1) one day

_____ (2) one week

_____ (3) one month

_____ (4) six months

_____ (5) one year

_____ (6) three years or more

C. Please circle the point on the scale provided which most nearly describes the frequency with which unanticipated or unprogrammed-for circumstances arise that would affect the unit's ability to perform its task effectively:

Very few unprogrammed or unanticipated circumstances   1   2   3   4   5   6   7   Very many unprogrammed or unanticipated circumstances

■

The external environment interview

By answering the following three sets of open-ended questions, the executives who responded to the external environment questionnaire also participated in individual interviews to clarify our understanding of the characteristics of the external environment:

1. What are the major strategic concerns of the unit? What are the determinants of success for the unit? On what basis would a customer or a client evaluate and choose between competing units in this business? On what basis or criteria do the managers above you evaluate the unit?

2. What are the major kinds of problems a unit such as this encounters in competing or surviving or succeeding in this business? How would you rank these problem areas in terms of (a) their criticalness to the success of the

unit, and (b) the difficulty in achieving effective resolution? What degree of coordination of work activities is required to succeed here?

3. In general, how routine and predictable are your unit's tasks? How programmable are they? What is the time-span of performance feedback?

Characteristics of Organization Unit Members

Tests to measure sense of competence

The presence and strength of individuals' feelings, attitudes, and expectations are very often assessed by behavioral scientists through some form of *projective* test. In such a test, a respondent is usually simply asked to write a story, complete a sentence, or give his reactions to ambiguous cues such as inkblots or unlabeled pictures. It is assumed that the individual *projects* into his responses his own thoughts, feelings, attitudes, and expectations, all of which can be scored from the content of the response. Many projective tests are some form of the Thematic Apperception Test (TAT) developed by Murray.[4] In the TAT, an individual is presented with a series of relatively ambiguous pictures of other individuals in social situations and he is asked to write an original and imaginative story suggested by each of the pictures in the set. With the help of two pilot tests, we developed our own TAT with a set of pictures to broadly suggest work or problem-solving situations, but we kept the pictures ambiguous enough to permit respondents to use their imagination in writing stories. Like most TATs, ours contained six pictures and allowed respondents about five minutes per picture to write a creative and imaginative story. The respondent had four questions to help him write his story. These and the instructions to the TAT follow.

■

An important asset in the business world is imagination—the capacity to think on your feet. This test gives you an opportunity to use your imagination, to show how you can create ideas and situations by yourself. In other words, instead of presenting you with answers already made up, from which you have to pick one, it gives you the chance to show how you can think things up on your own.

On the following pages you are to write out some brief stories that you make up on your own. In order to help you get started there are a series of pictures that you can look at and build your stories around. When you finish reading these instructions, you should turn the page, look at the first picture briefly, then

[4] H. A. Murray, *Explorations in Personality* (New York: Oxford University Press, 1938).

turn the page again and write a story suggested by the picture. To help you cover all the elements of a story plot in the time allowed, you will find four questions spaced out over the page. They are:

1. What is happening? Who are the people?
2. What has led up to this situation? That is, what has happened in the past?
3. What is being thought? What is wanted? By whom?
4. What will happen? What will be done?

Your overall time for each story is only 5 minutes. So plan to spend only about a minute on each of these questions, but remember that the questions are only *guides* for your thinking and need not be answered specifically in so many words. That is, the story should be continuous, not a set of answers to questions. Do not take over 5 minutes per story. You will be allowed only 30 minutes for this part of the test after you get started, although you may finish in less time if you like.

■

Do not worry about whether there are right and wrong kinds of stories to write because, in fact, any kind of story is all right. What you have a chance to show here is how you think on your feet, how quickly you can imagine a situation and write out a story about it. What story you write doesn't matter. So don't try to figure out exactly what is going on in the pictures. They are vague and suggest many things on purpose. Don't describe them. They are just to help give you an idea to write about.

Make your stories interesting and dramatic. Show that you have an understanding of human nature and can make up interesting stories about people, situations, and human relationships.

If you have read these instructions carefully and understood them, turn the page, look at the picture briefly, then turn the page again and write the story suggested to you by the picture. Don't take more than five minutes. Then turn the page, look at the next picture briefly, write out the story it suggests, and so on through the booklet.

■

Because of the importance of feelings of competence in this study, we also measured the respondents with a second projective technique, complementary to the TAT. This second test, based on the autobiographical format, gave individuals 30 minutes to write one creative and imaginative story.[5] Contrary to the TAT, there were no pictures to suggest story ideas. Rather, the individual was asked to write a story about his own work day in his organization "tomorrow," that is, "the day after today." By asking a person to be autobiographical and tell us about *his* work day, what *he* might be doing, thinking, or accomplishing, we expected that we would

---

[5] See, for example, Raphael S. Ezekiel, "The Personal Future and Peace Corps Competence," *The Journal of Personality and Social Psychology, Monograph Supplement* (February 1968):1-26, for an excellent and creative use of this method.

obtain stories potentially rich in feelings of competence and the expectation of being competent. The instructions for writing the "tomorrow's day" story were:

■

This second part of the test of imagination asks you to project yourself into the future and to organize your thoughts concerning the future into a concise, coherent, imaginative story. Consider "the future" here to be simply "tomorrow," that is, "the day after today." *Assume that you will be at your job in your organization tomorrow. Write a short story about your day in that organization tomorrow.* Tell what you may be thinking about, what may happen, what you may be doing, and what may be the outcomes of your day in terms of your feelings, frustrations, accomplishments, etc. You will have 30 minutes to compose your imaginative story of tomorrow's work day. As in Part I of this test, make your story interesting and dramatic.

■

Scoring the content of the stories for a sense of competence

To develop a scoring manual for measuring the respondent's sense of competence, we first listed a large number of dimensions indicative of an individual's feelings of competence that a researcher could observe in organization members' work activities or could score for in the content analysis of stories. We compared this list with those from other researchers who had attempted to measure a sense of competence.[6] What emerged from these two complementary steps was a comprehensive, simple scoring manual that operationalized feelings of competence in ongoing organizational situations.

We operationally defined *sense of competence* and subsequently scored the content of the stories in the *tests of imagination* along the five dimensions listed below, believing that an individual would be displaying feelings of competence to the extent which these dimensions were present in his stories:[7]

■

1. *Problem-solving orientation:* Does the person in the story solve recognized problems? For example, if the storywriter centers his story about the break-

[6] See, for example, Ezekiel, "The Personal Future," and George V. Coelho et al., "Use of the Student-TAT to Assess Coping Behavior in Hospitalized, Normal and Exceptionally Competent College Freshmen," *Perceptual and Motor Skills* 14 (1962): 355-365.

[7] These dimensions were also validated as operational measures of sense of competence in a personal conversation with Professor Emeritus Robert White.

down in a computer, does the "hero" in the story recognize the problem and put the equipment back in operating condition?

2. *Activity-influence orientation:* Does the person in the story actively perform or do things so as to solve problems? Continuing our example of a computer breakdown, is the person in the story described by the storywriter as turning dials, making adjustments, running test printouts, etc., so as to repair the computer?

3. *Knowledge of the task—or problem-solving situation:* Does the person in the story show that he clearly understands the terms and demands of the task or problem situation? For example, does the person working on the computer clearly indicate he knows what kinds of data should be coming out of the computer or what the probable causes of the breakdown are?

4. *Confidence orientation:* Does the storywriter depict the person in the story as feeling that he has the ability, the power, the "stuff" to solve the problem in the story? For example, is the hero above described as confident that he can have the breakdown "licked in no time?"

5. *Competence theme:* Does the story as a whole show the focal person in it to be the one who determines the course of events in the story? This is a judgment based on the content of the story as a whole, where the story in its entirety is evaluated as an elaboration of a theme showing feelings of competence.

■

Both of the projective tests were scored in exactly the same manner using these dimensions. Each thought or feeling could be used to score only one category, that is, the same idea in a story could not be used as an indication of more than one dimension. Each dimension could also be scored only once each per story in order to minimize the length of the story as a factor in our measurement.

The procedures used to insure objectivity and reliability of the scores for the test of imagination are well known, and we will only review them quickly. We first coded each test to indicate its source and then removed any other indications of the individual or the organization from which it came. Independent scorers, who did not know which questionnaires came from which unit, then shuffled protocols from all units together, scored all responses to one picture, reshuffled, scored all responses to the second picture and so on through the "tomorrow's day" story to give us a score and rescore for each protocol. We calculated the coefficient of correlation (r) between the score and rescore using the formula:

$$r = \frac{N\Sigma d_x d_y - \Sigma d_x \Sigma d_y}{\sqrt{N\Sigma d_x{}^2 - (\Sigma d_x)^2} \ \ \sqrt{N\Sigma d_y{}^2 - (\Sigma d_y)^2}}$$

where d_x is the score deviation in step intervals from an arbitrary origin on the X scale in a scatter diagram, and d_y is the same for the Y scale. We also measured the percentage of scoring imagery agreement between the score and rescore using the formula:

$$\frac{2 \ (\text{no. of agreements between score and rescore on the presence of imagery})}{\# \text{ of times first score imagery present} + \# \text{of times rescored imagery present}}$$

The sense of competence interview

In semistructured interviews with about half the respondents to our tests of imagination, we obtained clinical data about their feelings of competence through the following questions:

■

1. What are for you the major sources of stress or frustration in the unit, and what are the major sources of satisfactions or kicks for you in the unit (personal feelings concerning the external and internal environment)?
2. How confident would you say that people in your unit generally are concerning their ability to solve the unit's problems and accomplish its work? Do you more often hear feelings of frustration, anxiety, pessimism, uneasiness, etc. concerning the unit's work, or feelings of confidence, optimism, etc. concerning the work? How confident do you yourself feel regarding solving the unit's problems and accomplishing its tasks?

■

Measuring members' personality dimensions and predispositions

Schroder, et al. suggested that the level of individuals' integrative complexity could be assessed by scoring essays and related written materials.[8] They developed a seven-point scale, reproduced below, that we used to score the integrative complexity displayed in the essays written for the TATs and "tomorrow's day" projective tests. The scorers for integrative complexity were different from the scorers for feelings of competence. In fact, the former had no notions of any other prior use of the stories and essays, and they consistently found the stories appropriate vehicles for assessment. In scoring for integrative complexity, we followed the reliability and objectivity procedures originally employed in scoring for sense of competence. Protocols were scored and rescored by independent judges after coding and shuffling to ensure there would be no indication of the individual or the organization unit being measured. The coefficient of correlation between score and rescore was also calculated.

[8] H. M. Schroder, et al., *Human Information Processing,* pp. 200-201.

■

Scale Points Used for Assessing the Integrative Complexity
Involved in Essay Writing

Scale point	Description
1	Presents only one side of a problem. Ignores differences, similarities, and gradations.
2	One side of the problem presented and supported much more fully than the other. Opposing views perceived as compartmentalized or negative. No interrelationships considered.
3	Two or more views clearly differentiated. Similarities and differences implied or presented. One view can be opposed, but it is understood.
4	Includes all involved under scale point 3 but begins to "consider" the similarities and differences between views. At this level consideration is expressed . . . as qualifications of each . . . (e.g., "similar, but . . ."). That is, the simultaneous effects of alternate views become apparent in the writer's thinking.
5	Considers alternate and conflicting reasons for perceived similarities and differences between views in producing the essay.
6	Begins to consider relationships, not only among direct similarities and differences between sides of the problem, but also relationships between alternate reasons as to why the differences and similarities occur.
7	The consideration of notions which include relational linkages between alternate views. Such notions are open to all conflicting components and express attempts to see these as parts of a more inclusive "construction" of the problem.

■

We developed our own instrument to measure tolerance for ambiguity, attitudes toward authority, and attitudes toward working and being alone or with others. We scanned many generally accepted personality inventories (e.g., the Minnesota Multiphasic Personality Inventory, California Psychological Inventory, Kuder Preference Test) to abstract and derive a number of statements we felt were representative of these personality dimensions. To these, we added many value statements of our own invention to bring the number of statements up to 55. Using a factor analysis based on an orthogonal rotation on these data, we devised a 21 statement questionnaire to measure the three personality dimensions. The respondents in the study were given the following instructions for the instrument:

■

For each of the statements below, please draw a circle around:

DA—if you DEFINITELY AGREE; that is, if the statement definitely expresses how you feel about the matter.

IA—if you are INCLINED TO AGREE; that is, if you are not definite but think that the statement tends to express how you feel about the matter.

ID—if you are INCLINED TO DISAGREE; that is, if you are not definite, but think that the statement does *not* tend to express how you feel about the matter.

DD—if you DEFINITELY DISAGREE; that is, if the statement definitely does *not* express how you feel about the matter.

■

Each of the three dimensions contained positive and negative statements. Positive statements were scored:

■

DA	IA	ID	DD
4	3	2	1

■

and reflected the respondent's agreement with the item; negative statements were scored:

■

DA	IA	ID	DD
1	2	3	4

■

and reflected the respondent's disagreement with the item statement. The item statements used for the three dimensions are listed below:

■

Predisposition	*Questionnaire Items*
Tolerance for ambiguity (scored positive)	The most interesting life is to live under rapidly changing conditions.
	Off with the old, on with the new, even though a person rarely knows what the "new" will be.
	Adventurous and exploratory people go farther in this world than do systematic and orderly people.
	A really satisfying life is a life of problems. When one is solved, one moves on to the next problem.
Tolerance for ambiguity (scored negative)	It's satisfying to know pretty much what is going to happen on the job from day to day.
	When planning a vacation, a person should have ·a schedule to follow if he's really going to enjoy himself.

	Doing the same things in the same places for long periods of time makes for a happy life.
Attitude toward authority (scored positive)	Teachers who force students to use prescribed methods of study make it difficult for them to learn.
	The least possible governmental and social controls are best for all.
	One should welcome suggestions, but resent even reasonable orders.
	Even children know they must decide their actions; their fathers and mothers do not know best.
	Schools which force conformity stifle creativity.
Attitude toward authority (scored negative)	The best work is done with some close supervision.
	One often has to be told what to do in order to do a good job.
Attitude toward being and working alone or with others (scored positive)	If a person is satisfied with the kind of job he has done, he shouldn't get upset if colleagues criticize it.
	A person usually can get a job done faster and better by working alone than with a group.
	It's better to walk along a beach alone than to sit on a beach blanket with friends.
	A person gets more satisfaction out of reading an enjoyable book than from talking to friends about their vacation.
	One should never go with a group if the crowd means little to one.
Attitude toward being and working alone or with others (scored negative)	Others' thoughts of one's actions are of great importance.
	Even if a man loves a girl, he ought not to marry her if his friends don't approve of her.

■

The scores on these dimensions were combined into simple means, that is, all individual item scores for each dimension were added and then divided by the number of items.

The Internal Environment

The formal structure

We gathered information about the formal structure of the organizational units to gauge the degree of control and coordination achieved primarily through open-ended interviews with top company and unit executives. These executives were the same ones who also supplied us with interview and questionnaire data regarding characteristics of the external environment. The questions used to elicit interview data about the formal structure were:

■

1. Along what criteria or dimensions do you define job goals and position descriptions? How precisely defined are these job goals and position guides? How controlling are they?
2. How much reliance does your unit place on formal rules, operating policies, work and control and incentive procedures, and similar devices to guide employee behavior (including that of managers) in certain prescribed ways? What degree of coordination and control do they provide?
3. On what criteria or dimensions do you evaluate the performance of the unit as a whole? On what criteria do you evaluate the performance of individuals in the unit? How specific and controlling are these?
4. What kind of reporting cycle does the unit have? What kinds of reports come due with what frequency?
5. What general kinds of topics come up most often in the review sessions, the budget meetings, the meetings with superiors, the characteristic reports, etc. of the unit? What do you most often talk about in such meetings and what kinds of information do you most often find in such reports?

■

In addition to the information about the organizations' formal practices that was gathered from the interviews described above, we ourselves investigated organizational charts, position descriptions, procedural manuals, incentive and evaluation systems, etc. to get a better idea of each unit's formal structure and practices. Wherever possible, we also attended formal meetings, review sessions, planning conferences, etc. to observe how the formal practices were used. With this combination of data from the interviews, formal documents, and our own observations, we completed the "Researcher's Data Sheet for Unit Formal Practices" that follows. The first part of the data sheet defined and measured formality of structure in terms of the pattern of formal relationships and duties in an organization on the basis of average span of control, the number of levels in the hierarchy, the extent of the defined division of labor, and the specificity of job goals and position duties. The second part defined and measured the pattern of formal rules and procedures, on the basis of the importance of such formal items, the specificity of the criteria for the evaluation of both individual and organizational performance, and the areas of the organization that were subject to precise measurement, control, and coordination. The next section of the form was used to determine the time dimensions incorporated in the formal practices by scoring for the time-span of review of task performance, the shortest report period of organizational activities, and the characteristic time required to complete the unit's task or product and resource commitment time. The final section defined and measured the goal dimensions or the strategic concerns of formal practices from the content of formal reports, meetings, budgets, and goal statements in the organization. With the exception of *goal dimensions,* these aspects of the formal structure in an organization were scored on a four-point scale to describe the formal structure as shown below:

RESEARCHER'S DATA SHEET FOR UNIT FORMAL PRACTICES

(Data drawn from records, documents, charts, manuals, job descriptions, etc., and from interviews with top unit and company executives)

A score for each major variable is obtained by adding scores for all its subsidiary characteristics, except, as will be evident, for "Goal dimensions."

1. *The pattern of formal relationships and duties*   (low degree of structure ———➤ high degree)

	1	*2*	*3*	*4*
Average span of control	11-10 persons	9-8	7-6	5-3
Number of levels to a shared superior	7 or under	8-9	10-11	12 or over
Extent of defined division of labor	Only ill-defined roles	Some roles well-defined; most more open	Most roles well-defined; some left open	All roles clearly defined
Specificity of job goals and position duties	No job descriptions or position guides	General job descriptions and position guides for some jobs and positions	Specific descriptions and guides for most jobs and positions	Very specific descriptions and guides for all jobs and positions

2. *Formal rules, operating and work procedures, measurement/control systems, etc.*   (low degree of structure ———➤ high degree)

	1	*2*	*3*	*4*
Importance of formal rules	No rules	Rules on minor routine procedures	Comprehensive rules on routine procedures and/or limited rules on operations	Detailed rules on all routine operations and procedures
Specificity of criteria and standards for evaluation of role occupants	No formal evaluation	Formal evaluation; no fixed criteria	Formal evaluation; less than five criteria	Formal evaluation with detailed criteria
Specificity of review of unit performance	General oral review	General written review	One or more general statistics	Detailed statistics
Areas of the environment that are subject to precise measurement, control, and co-ordination	Very few	Some; a few	Quite a few; most	All

RESEARCHER'S DATA SHEET (*continued*)

3. *Time dimensions of formal practices* (long ⟶ short)

	1	2	3	4
Timespan of formal review of unit performance	More than 1 month	Monthly	Weekly	Daily
Timespan of shortest report period of unit activities	1 month or over	1-4 weeks	Weekly	Daily
Range of time over which employees can commit resources	6 months or over	1-6 months	Weekly	Daily
Characteristic "throughput" time, i.e., the timespan from beginning to completion of the usual unit task/ project/output	6 months or over	1-6 months	Weekly	Daily

4. *Goal dimensions of formal practices*

Content of characteristic reports from unit	Science	Techno-economic	Other
Content of review sessions of unit	Science	Techno-economic	Other
Content of budgeted monetary/physical items for unit, i.e., content of unit budgets	Science	Techno-economic	Other
Content of goal statements or definitions	Science	Techno-economic	Other

■

Members' own perceptions of the internal environment

Tests to measure members' perceptions
of the degree of control over work activities

To measure members' perceptions of the degree of structure, we abstracted two dimensions from Litwin and Myer's methodology to survey the *climate* in an organization.[9] These two were:

■

1. The "conformity" dimension, or the feelings that individuals had about constraints in the work organization and the degree to which they felt there were many rules, procedures, policies, and practices that they had to conform to, rather than being able to do their work as they saw fit; and,
2. The "organizational clarity" dimension, or the feeling that things were pretty well structured, rather than being disorderly and confused, and the degree to which things were felt to be well-defined and precisely structured.

■

Statements to elicit feelings and perceptions about these two structural dimensions were taken from a version of Litwin and Myer's climate questionnaire.[10] The administration and scoring of these aspects of the internal organizational environment followed the procedure described earlier to measure members' tolerance for ambiguity, attitude toward authority, and attitude toward working alone or with others.

The item statements for "conformity" and "organizational clarity" are listed below:

■

Conformity dimension
(scored positive)

Ordinarily we don't deviate from standard policies and procedures in this unit.

Excessive rules, administrative details, and red tape make it difficult for new and original ideas to receive consideration.

If you want to stay out of trouble around here, you have to conform to standard practices.

There are a lot of rules, policies, procedures, and standard practices one has to know to get along in this unit.

[9] Herbert H. Myer, "Achievement Motivation and Industrial Climates," in *Organizational Climate: Exploration of a Concept,* Renato Tagiuri and George H. Litwin, eds. (Boston: Harvard Business School, Division of Research, 1968).

[10] George H. Litwin; material was conveyed in a personal communication.

Conformity dimension (scored negative)	Our management isn't so concerned about formal organization and authority, but concentrates instead on getting the right people together to do the job.
	Unnecessary procedures are kept to a minimum in this unit.
Organizational clarity dimension (scored positive)	The assignments in this section are clearly defined.
	The policies and organization structure of this unit have been clearly explained.
	I feel I am a member of a clearly and precisely structured team.
Organizational clarity dimension (scored negative)	Things seem to be pretty disorganized around here.
	Our productivity sometimes suffers from lack of organization and structure.

■

The scores on these dimensions were combined into simple means, that is, all individual item scores for each dimension were added and then divided by the number of items. The "conformity" mean and the "organizational clarity" mean were then added together to obtain a final score for perceptions of the degree of structure and control in the unit's internal environment.

To gather data about supervisory style, we used a question developed in Miller's "Professionals in Bureaucracy: Alienation Among Industrial Scientists and Engineers," which is shown below: [11]

■

Which of the following statements most nearly represents the type of work relationship that exists between you and your superiors?

_____ 1. We discuss things a great deal and come to a mutual decision regarding the task at hand.

_____ 2. We discuss things a great deal and his decision is usually adopted.

_____ 3. We discuss things a great deal and my decision is usually adopted.

_____ 4. We don't discuss things very much and his decision is usually adopted.

_____ 5. We don't discuss things very much and I make most of the decisions.

[11] George A. Miller, "Professionals in Bureaucracy: Alienation Among Industrial Scientists and Engineers," *American Sociological Review* 32 (1967):755-768.

■

Items 1, 2, and 3 indicate a high rate of interaction between superiors and subordinates on decision-making matters and joint decision-making by superiors and subordinates, and, therefore, they were labeled as a *participatory* type of supervision. Item 4 indicates a low rate of interaction and unilateral decision-making by the superior, and was therefore scored as a *directive* type of supervision. Item 5 also indicates a low rate of interaction, but with most of the decisions being made by the subordinate; it was scored as a *laissez-faire* supervisory style.

We then asked participants to give us their perceptions of the amount of total influence being exercised in their unit and its distribution by indicating how much influence, ranging from 1 (little or no influence) to 5 (a very great deal of influence), various positions and groups had within the organization. Group and position titles were varied to suit each site, but the sample copy of the instructions below was uniform for all sites.

■

In general, how much say or influence do you feel each of the following groups or individuals has on the major problems that your unit faces? Please respond for your own unit using the scale provided below. You *may* use the same score to describe more than one group or position in your unit.

1. Little or no influence
2. Some influence
3. Quite a bit of influence
4. A great deal of influence
5. A very great deal of influence

■

With the influence scores, we determined the mean total influence perceived in the organization by averaging all the individual influence scores. We next determined, by fitting a line to the scores at each hierarchical level by regression analysis, how much average influence was perceived at various levels in the hierarchy.

Finally, to measure the amount of influence and control individuals perceived themselves to have in choosing and handling tasks on their own, we adapted the methodology of Pelz,[12] and Pelz and Andrews;[13] our adaptions follow.

[12] Donald C. Pelz, "Motivation of the Engineering and Research Specialist," *Improving Managerial Performance* (New York: American Management Association, Inc., 1957).
[13] Donald C. Pelz and Frank M. Andrews, *Scientists in Organizations: Productive Climates for Research and Development* (New York: Wiley, 1966).

■

In addition to differing in ways they think about those with whom they work, people can also differ in their ideas of the character of the relationship between them. We are interested in your description of the relationships between you and your colleagues and between you and your superiors in the unit: the following questions are intended to help you describe those relations. Please check the answers below that are most indicative of your ideas. Different aspects of your unit's tasks may require different kinds of relationships, so there are, of course, no "good" or "bad," "right" or "wrong" answers.

In general, with respect to your work supervisors in the unit, how much freedom or autonomy do you have to choose the type of task or project you will be involved in?

1. Almost no choice   _____

2. Very little choice   _____

3. Some choice   _____

4. A great deal of choice   _____

■

Once you have a task or project to work on, the freedom or autonomy that you have to run the job on your own can also vary. In your unit, to what degree can you handle the job on your own without having to check with your superiors every time a decision must be made?

1. Almost no freedom to handle the task on my own   _____

2. Very little freedom to handle the task on my own   _____

3. Some freedom to handle the task on my own   _____

4. A great deal of freedom to handle the task on my own   _____

■

Tests to Measure Members' Perceptions of Coordination of Work Activities

Perceptions of the degree of coordination of work behavior were gauged by the following items, all of which were adapted from the previously mentioned methodology of Pelz, and Pelz and Andrews.

■

The "approach' or "strategy" in tackling your unit's technical problems can vary, that is, at what point you start, what concepts or methods you use, what sequence of steps you follow, etc. When you are talking over a technical problem with your colleagues, to what extent do you find yourself adopting similar or different "technical strategies" or "approaches"?

1. Almost always different   _____

2. More often different than similar   _____

3. More often similar than different   _____

4. Almost always similar   _____

Each man comes to a work unit with his own previous experiences and background, that is, the kinds of units he has worked in before, the specialty skills he has developed, the kinds of problems he is familiar with, etc. How similar or different do you feel your current work colleagues and you are along these lines of previous experiences and background?

1. Almost completely different _____

2. More different than similar _____

3. More similar than different _____

4. Almost completely similar _____

Although a man will ordinarily have a number of work associates that he considers "colleagues," he will usually have one that he considers his most significant colleague. Try to single out such a person for yourself. How similar or different from this one most significant colleague would you consider: (a) your strategies for tackling a technical problem in your unit, and (b) your previous experiences and background?

	(a) Technical strategies	(b) Previous experience
1. Almost completely different	_____	_____
2. More different than similar	_____	_____
3. More similar than different	_____	_____
4. Almost completely similar	_____	_____

To what extent do members of your work group, headed by your immediate superior, coordinate their efforts for some common objective? Coordination of effort is:

1. Nil; each member's work is separate from the rest _____

2. Slight; for about one-quarter of the work _____

3. Moderate; for about half of the work _____

4. Substantial; for about three-quarters of the work _____

5. Full; almost all of the work within the group is coordinated _____

■

To measure the characteristic mode of resolving conflict to achieve required coordination in the sites, we followed Lawrence and Lorsch.[14] They used 25 aphorisms to represent the five modes of conflict resolution initially identified by Blake and Mouton, that is, confrontation, compromise, smoothing, forcing, and withdrawal.[15] From a factor analysis based on an orthogonal rotation, three factors were identified. We used only these three and the four aphorisms associated with each in our analysis.

[14] Lawrence and Lorsch, *Organization,* pp. 265-267.
[15] R. R. Blake and J. S. Mouton, *The Managerial Grid* (Houston: Gulf, 1964).

■

Factor and aphorisms

1. Forcing
   Might overcomes right.
   The arguments of the strongest always have the most weight.
   He who fights and runs away lives to run another day.
   If you cannot make a man think as you do, make him do as you think.

2. Smoothing
   Kill your enemies with kindness.
   Soft words win hard hearts.
   Smooth words make smooth ways.
   When one hits you with a stone, hit him with a piece of cotton.

3. Confrontation
   By digging and digging, the truth is discovered.
   Seek till you find and you'll not lose your labor.
   A question must be decided by knowledge and not by numbers, if it is to
   have a right decision.
   Come now and let us reason together.

■

Although we asked respondents for their ideas about the ideal way in
which conflict should be handled and the way it actually was handled in the
organization as shown below, we used only the latter in our analysis:

■

There is an old proverb that says, "It may be true what some men say; it must
be true what all men say." The problem in applying this to the way people work
together in organizational units is that all men do not say the same thing. Persons in any organization have different ways of dealing with their work associates on the job. The proverbs listed in the two questions below can be thought
of as descriptions of some of the different possibilities of resolving disagreements
as they have been stated in literature and in traditional wisdom.

1. You are asked to indicate *how desirable in your opinion* each of the proverbs
   listed below is as a way of resolving disagreements between members of your
   unit. Please use the following scores in evaluating the desirability of each
   proverb.
   1. Very desirable
   2. Desirable
   3. Neither desirable nor undesirable
   4. Undesirable
   5. Completely undesirable

Indicate your evaluation in the spaces below:

_____ 1. You scratch my back, I'll scratch yours.

_____ 2. When two quarrel, he who keeps silence first is the most praise-
worthy.

_____	3.	Soft words win hard hearts.
_____	4.	A man who will not flee will make his foe flee.
_____	5.	Come now and let us reason together.
_____	6.	It is easier to refrain than to retreat from a quarrel.
_____	7.	Better half a loaf than no bread.
_____	8.	A question must be decided by knowledge and not by numbers if it is to have a right decision.
_____	9.	When one hits you with a stone, hit him with a piece of cotton.
_____	10.	The arguments of the strongest always have the most weight.
_____	11.	By digging and digging, the truth is discovered.
_____	12.	Smooth words make smooth ways.
_____	13.	If you cannot make a man think as you do, make him do as you think.
_____	14.	He who fights and runs away lives to run another day.
_____	15.	A fair exchange brings no quarrel.
_____	16.	Might overcomes right.
_____	17.	Tit for tat is fair play.
_____	18.	Kind words are worth much and cost little.
_____	19.	Seek till you find, and you'll not lose your labor.
_____	20.	He loses least in a quarrel who keeps his tongue in cheek.
_____	21.	Kill your enemies with kindness.
_____	22.	Try and trust will move mountains
_____	23.	Put your foot down where you mean to stand.
_____	24.	One gift for another makes good friends.
_____	25.	Don't stir up a hornet's nest.

2. In answering this question you are asked to shift from *what is desirable* to *what actually happens* in your organization. As you read the proverbs below, please indicate, using the following scale, to what extent these proverbs describe behavior in your unit.

1. Describes very typical behavior which usually occurs.
2. Describes typical behavior which occurs frequently.
3. Describes behavior which occurs sometimes.
4. Describes untypical behavior which seldom occurs.
5. Describes behavior which never occurs.

Indicate your evaluation in the spaces below:

[The list was repeated.]

■

Tests to measure goal and time orientations
of individuals in the survey

The tool to measure the goal concerns of individuals gauged relative concerns for techno-economic, marketing, and scientific goals as follows:

■

In evaluating and considering the potentialities of a new idea, there are many considerations about which persons in different parts of the organization must be concerned. We recognize, while all of these concerns are important, that certain concerns will be most important to you. In order to learn which are most important in your personal opinion, we would like you to rank the criteria listed below as follows:

A. Place a *1* by the *five* criteria which are of most concern to you personally; and

B. Place a *2* by the *next five criteria* which are of *second* most concern to you personally.

Criteria

_____ The manufacturing costs associated with products resulting from the proposed idea. (techno-economic)

_____ Competition's response to products resulting from the proposed idea. (marketing)

_____ The potentialities for scientific publication which might result from the proposed idea. (scientific)

_____ The technical processing problems which might result from the proposed idea. (techno-economic)

_____ The contribution which research on the proposed idea might make to scientific knowledge. (scientific)

_____ The capability of the sales organization to sell a product resulting from the proposed idea. (marketing)

_____ The technical capability of the research staff to conduct research on the proposed idea. (scientific)

_____ The plant facilities which would be required for a product resulting from the proposed idea. (techno-economic)

_____ The effect of products resulting from the proposed idea on the sales of existing company products. (marketing)

_____ The problems of meeting delivery schedules on products resulting from the proposed idea. (techno-economic)

_____ The technical difficulty of developing a product resulting from the proposed idea to meet customer needs. (scientific)

_____ The market channels through which the product resulting from the proposed idea would be distributed. (marketing)

_____ The problems of scaling up a process for a product resulting from the proposed idea. (scientific)

_____ The price and volume at which a product coming from the proposed idea could be sold. (marketing)

_____ The difficulty of maintaining quality specifications on products stemming from the proposed idea. (techno-economic)

■

Orientations toward time were gathered from the following questions:

■

Persons working on different activities are concerned to differing degrees with current and future problems. We are here interested in learning how your time is divided between activities which will have an immediate effect on company profits and those which are of a longer-range nature. Indicate below what percentage of your time is devoted to working on matters which will show up in the organization's profit and loss statement within each of the periods indicated. Your answers should total 100 percent.

a. One month or less _____

b. One to three months _____

c. Three months to one year _____

d. One year to five years _____

100 percent

■

The internal environment interivew

Finally, to obtain added insights into members' perceptions of their internal environment within their unit, we conducted semistructured interviews with about half the study participants in each site. We used the open-ended questions below to obtain additional clinical data.

■

1. What are your primary or major concerns in your job? What are your objectives and goals in your job? What do you feel management rewards and evaluates you on? Are these the things that *should* be primary and major to you on your job? (goal and time orientation)

2. What kinds of relations between people do you see in the organization? What is it like working with others here? (perceptions of control, supervisory style, degree of coordination, mode of conflict resolution)

3. There are many aspects of a unit such as yours that the work is organized around, for example, formal practices, formal relationships and duties, rules, procedures, etc. Which of these *help* or *hinder* you in the performance of your job? How? Which would you change and how, so that you could do your job better? (perceptions of structure, control and coordination)

■

Index

76 77 9 8 7 6 5 4 3 2